The Pilgrim's Progress

A Readable Modern-Day Version of John Bunyan's *Pilgrim's Progress*
Part 1

Book by John Bunyan
Unabridged Revision by Alan Vermilye

BROWN CHAIR BOOKS
BOOKS THAT INSPIRE

The Pilgrim's Progress
A Readable Modern-Day Version of John
Bunyan's *Pilgrim's Progress*
Part 1

Copyright © 2020 Alan Vermilye
Brown Chair Books

ISBN-13: 978-1-948481-12-0

To learn more about this book and the Bible study resources that go with it, to order additional copies, or to download the answer guide, visit **www.BrownChairBooks.com**.

Version 3

Contents

Acknowledgements

I would like to thank my wife Sherry who encouraged me to create this revision while also believing that I could do it, my reviewer team who provided valuable edits and feedback, and John Bunyan for writing such an influential and excellent book.

Introduction

I always had good intentions to read *The Pilgrim's Progress* by John Bunyan. Sure, it's a classic and probably every Christian should read it, but each time I tried, I felt as though I needed a 16th century translator. So I would give up, only to try again later with the same results.

While trying to decide my next Bible study project, my wife challenged me to consider *The Pilgrim's Progress*. I agreed that it was a good idea, but if I was to create a study, it would only make sense that I would also need to create a more readable version of the book. Surely if I struggled reading it, others did too. And what would be the purpose of creating a study for a book that people could not understand?

With much enthusiasm, I charted out my work. Normally, I can complete one of my studies in about four months, so I figured a project of this magnitude should take no more than six or eight months max. A year and a half later, and who knows how many hours, I finally published what I consider my opus!

Why so long? For one, all my projects require a lot of research, but this one took considerably more both for the book and the study.

Secondly, I discovered that taking Bunyan's original text and interpreting it for the modern-day reader was more challenging than I had thought. My most important consideration was to convert this antiquated text into simple conversational English without being unfaithful to the original. In fact, if you compare my version with the original, you will find no key element missing.

What you will find is sentence construction and certain interpretations of character reactions modified or enhanced to produce a more contemporary style of expression without sacrificing the intrinsic message.

Also, instead of using the archaic term "stages" to separate book sections, you will find chapter headings and subdivisions. I also retained the marginal scriptural references included by Bunyan.

Yes, it's true, every Christian should probably read *The Pilgrim's Progress*. Why? Because it's the spiritual journey of every believer, from our first conviction until the moment we enter heaven, told in the most brilliant of allegories.

I sincerely hope that my earnest rendering of this beloved classic will make this message as clear for you as it has been for me.

The Bible Study Guide

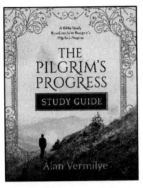

The Pilgrim's Progress Study Guide is a 12-week Bible study that was created specifically for this book.

Perfect for small groups or individual study, each weekly study session applies a biblical framework to the concepts found in each chapter and subsection of the book. Although intriguing and entertaining, much of Bunyan's writings can be difficult to grasp.

The Pilgrim's Progress Study Guide will guide you through Bunyan's masterful use of metaphors to a better understanding of the key concepts of the book, the supporting Bible passages, and the relevance to our world today. Each study question is ideal for group discussion, and answers to each question are available online.

You will also find commentary, character and places summaries, discussion questions for each section, and complete answers to all questions available for free online.

You can find retailers in order to purchase this book at www.BrownChairBooks.com.

Chapter One

Fleeing the City of Destruction

As I walked through the wilderness of this world, I came to a place where there was a clearing, and I laid down in it to sleep.

While I slept, I dreamed about a man in ragged clothes who stood, with his face turned away from his own house and with a book in his hand, carrying a great burden on his back. I saw him read from the pages of the book, weeping and shaking in fear until eventually he cried out loudly, "What should I do?"[1]

He anxiously returned home and tried to remain calm so that his wife and children would not become worried. But he became so distressed that he could no longer be silent and decided it was time to tell his family exactly what was on his mind.

"I love you all dearly," he said to his wife and children, "but I feel I must share with you this miserable and heavy burden that I've been carrying. You see, I've been reading this book and learned that our town will be destroyed—burned with fire from heaven—and unless we find some way to escape, all of us will die."

His family and friends were all amazed with his story, not because they believed him but rather because they considered

---

[1] Isa. 64:6; Luke 14:33; Psalm 38:4; Acts 2:37, 16:30; Hab. 1:2–3

him sick or even losing his mind. As evening approached, they were confident that a good night's sleep was all he needed to settle down, so they quickly got him to bed.

When morning came, they asked how he was feeling, and he said, "It's worse than before." He wanted to share with them more about what he had learned in the book, but they would not listen. Sometimes they spoke harshly to him, and at other times they laughed. Eventually they just ignored him.

He was sad, so he withdrew to his room and prayed for them while nursing his own grief. For weeks, he would go out alone into the woods and fields to read his book and pray.

One day, as he was walking in the fields, he became so distressed that he cried out, "Who will save me?"[2]

He thought that perhaps he should run, but to where should he run? As he stood there in misery, not knowing what to do, a man named Evangelist walked up to him and asked calmly, "Why are you crying?"

"Sir, I've been reading this book," he replied, "and I now realize that I'm condemned to die and after that, God will judge me. I find that I'm not willing to do the first nor able to do the second. Now I fear dying."[3]

Evangelist responded, "Why do you fear dying since this life is full of evil?"

The man answered, "Because I fear this burden on my back is too heavy and will make me sink lower than the grave until I fall into Hell! If I'm not fit to die, then I'm sure that I'm not fit to go to judgment and from there to execution. When I think of these things, it makes me cry."[4]

"If this is your condition, why are you still standing here?"

[2] Acts 16:30–31
[3] Heb. 9:27, Job 10:21–22, Ezek. 22:14
[4] Isa. 30:33

asked Evangelist.

The man shrugged his shoulders and said, "Because I don't know where to go!"

Evangelist handed him a scroll with these words on it: "Flee from the wrath to come!"[5]

The man read it and asked, "But where should I flee to?"

There was a wide field before them with a gate. "Do you see that wicket gate?" Evangelist asked.[6]

The man looked far into the distance and said, "No, I do not."

Evangelist asked, "How about the light? Do you see the light?"[7]

The man looked closer and said excitedly, "Yes, I think I do!"

"Good! Keep that light in your eye, and go straight to it," said Evangelist. "When you arrive at the gate, knock, and you will be told what you are to do."

Then I saw in my dream that Christian—for that was the man's name—set off running to the gate.

---

[5] Matt. 3:7
[6] Matt. 7:13–14
[7] Psalm 119:105, 2 Pet. 1:19

In Pursuit of Christian

Now, Christian had not gone far from his own home when his wife and children came out running, pleading and begging him to come back home, but he put his hands to his ears and ran on, crying, "Life! Life! Eternal life!" He never looked behind him but ran toward the middle of the field.[8]

His neighbors also came out to see him run. As he ran, some mocked, others threatened, and some cried after him to return. Two of the neighbors, Obstinate and Pliable, set off to bring him back, by force if necessary. By this time, Christian was a good distance ahead of them, but they were determined to catch him and eventually did.[9]

Christian turned to the men and asked, "Why have you come after me?"

The men had to stop and catch their breath from running so hard. "We have come to persuade you to return with us."

But Christian stood his ground. "I can no longer live in the City of Destruction. I was born and raised there, but now I know what kind of city it is. My eyes have been opened, and I know the truth. Why don't you both come with me? Otherwise you will die in this city and sink down below the grave into a place that burns with fire."

---

[8] Luke 14:26, Gen. 19:17
[9] Jer. 20:10

"What?" Obstinate said, astonished. "And leave our families and the comforts of life behind us?"

"Yes," said Christian. "Everything that you leave behind will not even compare to the smallest portion of what I'm seeking to enjoy. If you come with me and persevere, you'll find more than enough. I'm telling you the truth. Come with me and see!"[10]

Obstinate was curious and asked, "What are the things you are searching for that can't be found in this world?"

"I'm searching for a joy that does not fade," replied Christian, "a secure inheritance in Heaven that cannot be corrupted and will be given at the appointed time to those who earnestly search for it." He held out the book in his hand. "Don't take my word for it. Read it in my book."[11]

Obstinate threw up his hands and quickly dismissed Christian. "Nonsense! Put away your foolish book. Are you coming back with us or not?"

Christian shook his head. "No, I will not. I've put my hand to the plow and will not turn back."[12]

Obstinate motioned to Pliable. "Let's go home without him, Pliable. There's no convincing a fool once they believe themselves wiser than all their family and friends."

But Pliable did not move. Instead, he seemed to be considering Christian's offer. "Let's not be too quick to judge Christian," said Pliable. "If he's telling the truth, then what he's searching for is far more valuable than anything we have here. I think I'm inclined to go with him."

Obstinate was dumbfounded. "What? You can't be serious! Don't follow a fool like him. Come back with me."

---

[10] 2 Cor. 4:18, Luke 15:17
[11] 1 Peter 1:4, Heb. 11:16
[12] Luke 9:62

"Don't listen to him," Christian urged Pliable. "Come with me, and you'll discover the things that I just spoke of and so much more too!" He extended the book to Pliable. "Read the truth for yourself in this book that has been fully confirmed with the blood of Him who wrote it."[13]

Pliable did not take the book but instead looked at his friend Obstinate and said, "I think that I will go along with Christian and share my fate with his." He then turned excitedly to Christian and said, "Do you know the way to this glorious place?"

"I've been told by a man named Evangelist to hurry to that little gate in front of us, where we will receive further instructions and will be told how to find the Way."

Pliable was enthusiastic. "What are we waiting for? Let's get going!"

While the two of them took off together as fast as they could for the gate, Obstinate stood in disbelief and yelled after them, "I'm going back home and refuse to be misled by you fools!"

---

[13] Heb. 9:17–21

A Conversation with Pliable

In my dream, I saw Obstinate go back home while Christian and Pliable set off to cross the field, talking as they went.

"Pliable, I'm so happy that you decided to come with me," said Christian. "If Obstinate could only understand the dangers and terrors that await him, he would not have turned his back on us so easily."

"I'm sure that's true. Now, Christian," pressed an eager Pliable, "since it's just the two of us, tell me more about all the things we will find in our search."

Christian once again reached for his book. "I can understand it in my head, but for some reason, I find it difficult to talk about. However, I know I can find the answers to all your questions in this book."

"And you're confident the words in your book are true?" asked Pliable, pointing to Christian's book.

"Absolutely!" said Christian without hesitation. "The book was made by Him who cannot lie."[14]

"That's good enough for me! So tell me more about these things in your book."

Christian eagerly began, "The book tells us of a world with no boundaries and a life that never ends."[15]

---

[14] Titus 1:2
[15] Isa. 65:17, John 10:27–29

"Amazing! What else does it say?"

"It says that we will receive a crown of glory and robes that will make us shine like the sun!"[16]

"That's incredible! Does it say anything else?"

"Yes! That we'll never grieve again and that the King of the place will wipe every tear from our eyes."[17]

"Wonderful!" replied Pliable. Then he paused and grew concerned. "But who will we meet there, and what will they be like?"

"We will be met by angels and tens of thousands of all the saints in robes so bright that our eyes will dazzle just to look at them! There will be those that have gone before us in this world and have stood for the faith and suffered greatly, including being burned on the stake, thrown to wild beasts, and drowned in the seas—all because of their love for the Lord. They will not harm us but will greet us with love because they walk with God."[18]

Although fascinating, it did not seem to alleviate Pliable's concern. "That's all very interesting, but what will be our share in all of this, and what will it cost?"

"The Lord of that land has promised that if we are truly willing to receive our inheritance, He will give it to us freely,"[19] explained Christian.

Pliable let out a sigh of relief. "This is very good news, Christian! Come on. Let's pick up our pace and get there quicker."

"I'm trying," said Christian, moving as fast as he could, "but this load on my back slows me down."

---

[16] 2 Tim. 4:8, Rev. 22:5, Matt. 13:43
[17] Isa. 25:8; Rev 7:16–17, 21:4
[18] Isa. 6:2; 1 Thess. 4:16–17; Rev. 4:4, 5:11, 14:1–5; John 12:25; 2 Cor. 5:2
[19] Isa. 55:12; John 6:37, 7:37; Rev. 21:6, 22:17

Battling the Swamp of Despair

As they were talking, Christian and Pliable drew near to a very muddy swamp, named Despair, in the middle of the field. Since neither were paying any attention to where they were going, they both fell in. They battled in the swamp for some time totally covered in mud, and the load that Christian carried on his back made him sink even more.

Looking around, Pliable asked, "Christian, where are we now?"

"Truthfully, I have no idea!" Christian said, struggling to find a way out.

Offended, Pliable angrily asked, "Is *this* the happiness that you've been telling me about all this time? If this is what happens at the beginning of our journey, I cannot imagine what we can expect to find at the end. If I get out of this mess with my life, I'm going home, and you can travel to your noble country without me!"

And with that, he gave a desperate struggle or two and climbed out of the mud on the side of the swamp nearest to his home, and Christian never saw him again.

So Christian was left to battle his way through the Swamp of Despair on his own, without any help. He formulated a plan and decided his best option was to reach the side of the swamp closest to the Wicket Gate, in the opposite direction from his home. He slowly inched his way across the muddy swamp until he finally reached the edge but then found that he could not get out because of the heavy burden on his back.

Then I saw in my dream a man, whose name was Help, came to him and asked him, "What are you doing here?"

"A man called Evangelist gave me directions to the Wicket Gate so that I could escape the destruction that's coming to my city. As I started heading to the gate, I fell in here."

"But why didn't you look for the steps to cross the swamp?" Help asked him.

"I'm afraid that I was in such a hurry that I did not see them and fell right in," Christian admitted, feeling a little embarrassed.

Help reached out to Christian. "Give me your hand, and I will pull you out." And with that, Help pulled Christian out of the swamp and set him on solid ground, wishing him well.[20]

Then, in my dream, I approached Help and asked him, "Excuse me, sir. Since this place is on the way from the City of Destruction to the Wicket Gate, why has no one repaired this patch of ground to keep those who come by from falling into the swamp?"

And he said to me, "This swamp cannot be fixed. Since it's a low-lying plot of land, all sorts of scum and filth associated with the conviction of sin drain into it. Therefore it's called the Swamp of Despair. As a traveling sinner becomes aware of their own lost condition, doubts and fears arise in their mind, and then it all drains down and settles in this place. This is what makes the ground so bad.

"The King never intended that this place should remain in such bad condition," he said. "For this very reason, His workers have been attempting to repair this ground in

---

[20] Psalm 40:2

accordance to the direction of His Majesty's surveyors for over two thousand years. To the best of my knowledge, this swamp has swallowed up at least twenty thousand cart-loads, which equates to millions of wholesome instructions that have been brought from all regions of the King's dominions in all seasons. It has been said that these were the best materials possible to make solid ground, but even so, the Swamp of Despair remains after they did all they could.[21]

"The Lawgiver has provided a number of reliable and solid steps placed in the middle of the swamp, but it's hard to see them for all the filth. In cases where the weather changes, the steps are hardly visible. Even when men do notice the steps, they often miss them on account of guilt-induced dizziness. But the ground is good when they enter the gate."[22]

Now, in my dream, Pliable had gone back home. Some of his friends called him wise for coming back home, while others said he was a fool to have gone in the first place. Others just mocked him and called him a coward for giving up too easily when encountering a few difficulties.

Pliable did his best to stay away from them, and that was when he noticed that they had all turned their taunts and laughter to poor Christian. However, that's enough concerning Pliable.

---

[21] Isa. 35:3–4
[22] 1 Sam. 12:23

The Advice of Worldly Wiseman

Alone once again, Christian continued his journey, walking through the field until he spotted a man coming up to meet him. The man introduced himself as Mr. Worldly Wiseman from the large town of Carnal Policy, not too far from Christian's own home. He had become well acquainted with the rumors circulating of Christian's escape from the City of Destruction. As he approached Christian, he noticed him groaning and struggling and said, "Say there, friend, where are you going with that heavy burden on your back?"

"Yes, it *is* a heavy burden! Probably greater than anyone has had to carry," said Christian. "If you must know, I'm heading to that wicket gate over there because I've been told that's where I can get it removed."

"Do you have a wife and children?" Worldly Wiseman asked.

Sadly, Christian said, "Yes, I do, but since I've been carrying this heavy burden, I no longer find pleasure in them as I once did. In fact, sometimes I feel as though I have no family at all."[23]

"I would like to give you some great advice if you will listen to me," prompted Worldly Wiseman, leaning into Christian.

---

[23] 1 Cor. 7:29

"If it's good advice, I will listen because, quite honestly, I need some," replied Christian.

"Then I would tell you to get rid of that burden on your back as quickly as possible! You will never be able to rest and experience the blessing that God has in store for you until you do."

"That's exactly what I'm trying to do!" said Christian. "But I cannot seem to get rid of it by myself, and I've found no one else who can help me with it either. That's why I'm heading to that gate, as I told you before, so that I can get rid it."

Worldly Wiseman's eyebrows raised. "Who told you that going to that gate would get rid of your burden?"

"A very great and honorable man. If I recall, his name was Evangelist."

Worldly Wiseman grimaced. "Oh, that man. He's a terrible guide and has given you the most dangerous advice possible. It should be obvious to you. Just look at the mud from the Swamp of Despair on your clothes. Trust me, that swamp is just the beginning of your problems. I'm older and more experienced, and I guarantee that if you continue on this path, you'll be met with pain, sadness, hunger, nakedness, lions, dragons, darkness, and, yes, the sword too. In a word—death! I'd advise you not to listen to this man Evangelist."

"I appreciate your advice, but I don't think you quite understand," replied Christian. "This burden on my back is worse than all of the things you just mentioned. Right now, I really don't care who or what I meet along the way as long as I can get rid of it."

Pointing to Christian's back, Worldly Wiseman asked, "Tell me, how did you get your burden in the first place?"

Christian lifted his book up. "I found it by reading this book."

"I thought so," said Worldly Wiseman, nodding. "I've seen

this sort of thing before in other weak men. Just like you, they begin to learn about teachings too difficult for them to understand, and in no time, they're confused. Eventually they begin to suffer and humiliate themselves by searching for desperate measures to cure themselves without a clue as to what will happen."

"That might be true for some," replied Christian, "but I know exactly what I'm looking for—relief from this burden."

"But why are you seeking relief like this when it's so dangerous? If you can be patient and listen, I will tell you exactly how to find what you're looking for—and risk free at that! In fact, my way is not only closer and less dangerous but you'll find safety, friendship, and happiness."

Christian was open to hearing more and begged, "Please, sir, tell me your secret!"

"Absolutely!" Pointing off in a different direction from the wicket gate, he said, "Why, just a short distance away is the Village of Morality. When you get there, ask for a gentleman named Legality. Now, he has excellent judgment and a great reputation and is renowned for helping men remove their burdens.

"Not just that—he's also skilled in curing the anxieties that accompany burdens. If I were you, I would go to him right now. You'll find his house no less than a mile from here. If he's not home, ask for his son, Civility. He's also quite pleasant and will be able to help you, just like his father can. If you go, I assure you that your burden will be removed in no time."

Worldly Wiseman continued, "Afterward, if you still choose not to go home, you can send for your wife and children to come live with you in the village. You'll find many wonderful homes that are empty and available but reasonably priced. In fact, the overall standard of living is very inexpensive. It's the perfect environment to raise a family, find honest neighbors, and create a financially secure and attractive future."

Now Christian was not sure what to do, but after thinking it over for some time, he decided it was best to trust the advice of Worldly Wiseman. "So," Christian said, eager to get started, "how do I get to this man's house?"

"Do you see that hill?" asked Worldly Wiseman, pointing off in the distance.

"Yes, I do."

"Go directly to that hill, and the first house you come to is his."

So Christian left the path to the Wicket Gate and set out on a new path to find Mr. Legality and finally get his burden removed.

In Search of Morality

Christian left the narrow Way and ventured out to find Mr. Legality for help with his burden, but the closer he got to the hill, which seemed more like a mountain, the harder it was to go up. In fact, the hill rose so high that it seemed to hang above him. He became paralyzed with fear and did not know what to do. His burden, too, seemed to weigh more now than it did when he was on the path to the Wicket Gate.

Then suddenly flames of fire burst out from the side of the mountain. Christian began to sweat and became deathly afraid of being burned.[24]

He thought, *Why did I ever listen to Worldly Wiseman?* Just then he spotted Evangelist coming his way. He was relieved but at the same time embarrassed since he had ignored the man's advice.

As Evangelist drew closer, Christian could tell that he was disappointed. "What are you doing here?" Evangelist asked.

Christian did not know what to say, so he said nothing. Evangelist continued, "Aren't you Christian, the man whom I found crying outside the City of Destruction?"

Christian dared not look up but said, "Yes, I'm he."

"I'm sorry," Evangelist said. "Did I not point you to the

---

[24] Ex. 19:16, 18; Heb. 12:21

Way that leads to the Wicket Gate?"

"Yes, you did."

"Then I'm confused. How is it that you have ended up here, so far off the Way?"

"After I got out of the Swamp of Despair, I met a gentleman who told me about another man in the Village of Morality who could quickly remove my burden," Christian said, glancing up at Evangelist.

"Who was he, and what did he look like?"

"He looked like a gentleman," replied Christian. "At first I wanted to stay on the Way to the gate, but he was very persuasive and finally convinced me that his way was best. When I got to this mountain, however, and saw how steep it was, I froze, thinking it might fall on me at any moment."

Evangelist inquired of Christian further. "Tell me exactly what this gentleman said to you."

"He asked me where I was going, and I told him."

"Then what did he say?"

"He asked me if I had a family. I told him yes and that I've not been able to enjoy them as before, especially since I've been carrying around this burden on my back."

Evangelist continued to probe. "Tell me more."

"He suggested that I should get rid of my burden as quickly as I could." Then Christian finally looked up. "I told him that's exactly what I'm trying to do by going to the Wicket Gate— to get relief. But he claimed he knew a better way, one that was shorter and less difficult than the way you recommended. His way would take me to the house of a man who is skilled at removing burdens."

Christian looked down again. "So I believed him and turned from your Way to his, hoping it would be better. But when I got here and realized that things were not as he promised, I stopped because I knew I was in danger. Now I don't know what to do."

"I want you to calm down and listen to me for a moment," said Evangelist, "so that I can show you the words of God."

Christian stood shaking in expectation of what Evangelist might say.

Evangelist began reading from the book: "See that you do not refuse godly advice just like the nation of Israel did. For if God's own people did not escape judgment and suffered for it, how much more will you suffer if you turn away from Him who warns you from heaven. And what's more, He tells us that if we are His, we will live by faith, but if we turn our backs on Him, our souls will suffer without Him.[25]

"Christian, you're the man running into this suffering," Evangelist said, pointing at him. "You have rejected God's counsel by going in a different direction from the way of peace, even to the point of eternally losing your life."

Christian fell face down and began to cry aloud, "What have I done? I'm ruined now!"

But Evangelist caught him by the right hand and said, "Men will be forgiven for their sins and indiscretions. Don't be like someone with no faith—you need to start believing!" This gave Christian some hope, and he stood back up, still shaking.[26]

Evangelist continued, "Now please pay attention and believe what I'm going to tell you about this man who has fooled you. Mr. Worldly Wiseman, as he is commonly known, delights in worldly thinking so much that he believes it will save him from the cross. Why do you think he attends the church of Morality? And it's because of his worldly attitude

---

[25] Heb. 10:38, 12:25,
[26] Matt. 12:31, John 20:27

that he tries to oppose me and the work of God.[27]

"There are three things in the man's advice that you must absolutely hate: first, his cunning ability to turn you away from the true path; secondly, his work in displaying the cross as unpleasant and repulsive; and finally, that he points you in a direction that ultimately leads to death."

Feeling that Christian needed further explanation, Evangelist continued, "Let's talk more about each one of these things. As I said, first you must be cautious of his ability to turn you away from the true path, even though you consented for a time. Why would you listen to the advice of Worldly Wiseman rather than that of God? The Lord tells us to go through the straight gate, the gate to which I sent you, because that gate leads to life. Unfortunately, few ever find it. This wicked man easily turned you away from the gate that leads to life and instead led you almost to destruction. You should be disappointed in yourself for ever listening to him.[28]

"Secondly, he will try to convince you that the cross is detestable, but you should prefer it more than all the treasures of Egypt. Besides, the King of Glory has said that if you wish to save your life, you must be willing to lose it. And if you follow Him but do not hate your father, mother, wife, children, brothers, sisters, and even your own life, you cannot be His disciple. Think about it like this: Worldly Wiseman wants to convince you that God's way will lead to suffering and death, but the truth is that you cannot have eternal life without following God's way. Therefore, you must strongly reject Worldly Wiseman's teachings.[29]

"Finally, you must hate the fact that the directions he gave you lead to death. Let's talk more about this man, Legality,

---

[27] 1 John 4:5, Gal. 6:12
[28] Luke 13:24, Matt. 7:13–14
[29] Heb. 11:25–26, Mark 8:38, John 12:25, Matt. 10:39, Luke 14:26

who supposedly would help you. This man is actually the son of a bondswoman who is in bondage along with her children."

Evangelist pointed to the hill that had overpowered Christian. "You see, this bondswoman represents Mount Sinai, which is the mountain you feared would fall on your head. Now, if she and all her children are in bondage, how do you expect them to help you? You thought that Legality could provide you an easier route to get what you wanted, but he has never helped any man get rid of his burden nor will he ever, regardless of what Mr. Worldly Wiseman tells you."[30]

Evangelist placed his hand on Christian's shoulder. "The fact is, no man has ever been able to get rid of his own burden nor can he expect the moral law will do so either. Mr. Worldly Wiseman is a liar, and Mr. Legality is a cheat. As for his son, Civility, he is just a hypocrite and no better. Believe me, there's no substance in anything these foolish men say. Their only aim is to cheat you of your salvation and turn you from following the true way that I have told you about."

After this, Evangelist called aloud to the heavens for confirmation of what he had just said, and immediately words and fire came out of the mountain just over where Christian was standing, which made every hair on his body stand on end. Then he heard the following words: "Those who rely on the works of the law are under the curse. For it is written, cursed is everyone who doesn't continue to obey every command written in the Book of the Law."[31]

Christian now expected death, so he began to cry out and curse the moment he ever met Mr. Worldly Wiseman, calling himself a thousand fools for even listening to his lies. He was ashamed that he had been swayed so easily by bad advice coming from human reasoning and that he would turn his back

---

[30] Gal. 4:21–27
[31] Gal. 3:10

so easily on the right way.

Christian lifted his head, in tears. "Is there any hope for me, Evangelist? Would it be possible for me to go back on the Way and continue through the Wicket Gate? Or am I now stuck forever in my shame of disobedience? I'm so sorry that I listened to this man's lies. Can my sin ever be forgiven?"

Drawing him near, Evangelist looked him directly in the eyes and said, "Your sin is very great because you have committed two evils: You abandoned the right way and then chose to follow a forbidden path. Yet the man at the Wicket Gate will still receive you because he has goodwill for men. However, make sure that you do not turn away from the Way again or it could likely be your demise as God's anger might burn against you!"[32]

Then Christian committed to returning to the narrow Way. Evangelist then kissed him and encouraged him with a smile, saying, "God be with you, Christian!"

---

[32] Psalm 2:12

Chapter Two

Arrival at the Wicket Gate

Christian left in a hurry and did not speak to anyone on the road, not even if someone asked him a question. He knew it was not safe until he reached the path he had left after receiving Worldly Wiseman's bad counsel.

At last he arrived at the Wicket Gate and found a sign over it that read, "Knock and it will be opened for you."[33]

With his hands trembling, he eagerly knocked several times, asking, "Can I enter here? Will the One who is inside allow me in the gate even though I'm an undeserving rebel? If you take me in, I will sing His praises forever!"

At last a very serious and grave-looking man came to the gate, whose name was Goodwill. "Who's there?" he asked. "And where are you from?"

"My name is Christian, and I'm a poor, burdened sinner," he replied. "I come from the City of Destruction, but I'm going to the Celestial City to escape the wrath that's coming. I've been told, sir, that the Way is through this gate. Will you let me in?"

"I'm willing with all my heart," he said, and with that,

---

[33] Matt. 7:7

Goodwill flung open the gate.

As he was stepping in, Goodwill reached out and clutched Christian's hand, yanking him through the gate.

Christian was both surprised and startled. "Why did you do that?"

Peering outside the gate, Goodwill said, "A short distance from here stands a well-fortified castle where Beelzebub directs his demons, equipped with flaming arrows, to shoot to kill anyone who comes to this gate hoping to enter."

"That's frightening! But I'm very grateful to you," Christian said, relieved that he was safely inside the gate.

Goodwill turned his attention back to Christian. "Who told you to come this way?"

"Evangelist told me to come this way and to knock at the gate. He then said you could tell me what to do next. So that's why I'm here."

"An open door is before you, and no man can shut it!" responded Goodwill.

Christian was relieved. "Now I can begin to reap the benefits of all the risk I took to get here."

Goodwill motioned behind Christian. "But why did you come alone?"

Shrugging his shoulders, Christian said, "Because none of my family or friends recognized the danger we were in like I did."

"Did they all know that you were leaving home to come here?'

"Yes, my wife and children saw me go." He paused for a moment, looking off into space, and said, "I heard them crying for me as I started to run, but they could not stop me. Some of my friends wanted me to come home too, but I refused to listen to them and came here alone."

Goodwill asked, "Did any of them chase after you and beg you to come back home?"

"Oh, to be sure!" Christian said. "My two neighbors, Obstinate and Pliable, did come after me. Once they figured out there was no convincing me to return, Obstinate went home, but Pliable came with me as far as the Swamp of Despair."

"Why is Pliable not with you now?" Goodwill asked, looking around.

"Well, we did come together, that is, until we got to the Swamp of Despair and both suddenly fell in. Pliable, as good of a friend as he is, became discouraged and refused to go any farther. Without much difficulty, he was able to get out of the swamp next to his home. He then told me to go find the brave country alone on his behalf. So he returned, following Obstinate, and I came to this gate."

"Oh, that poor man!" Goodwill said, shaking his head. "Did he think so little of the glories of Heaven that it was not worth a few risks to gain it?"

"Yes, you could say that's true of Pliable, but I'm really not any better," Christian said, hanging his head in shame. "Oh sure, he went back to his own house, but I also turned back to go and almost lost my life after being persuaded by the foolish arguments of Mr. Worldly Wiseman."

"Oh, he preyed upon you too, did he?" said Goodwill. "I'm assuming he suggested that Mr. Legality could rid you of your burden. Truth be told, they're both cheats. But don't tell me that you listened to him?"

"Unfortunately, I did," said Christian. "I set out to find Mr. Legality, but when the mountain that stands by his house seemed as though it would fall on me, I immediately stopped!"

"That mountain has been the death of so many and will likely be the death of many more," Goodwill said. "You're fortunate to have escaped it without being smashed to pieces."

"Honestly, I'm not sure what would've happened to me on that mountain had Evangelist not arrived when he did. I was moping around feeling sorry for myself, and by God's mercy, he was more than willing to help me again. If he hadn't, I never would've made it here."

Then Christian looked from Goodwill to the land before him. "But I'm here now, more fit for death by that mountain than to be standing here talking with my Lord. Oh, I'm so grateful that you let me in here!"

"We don't object to anyone who knocks at this gate and wants to come in, regardless of what they did before coming here, and in no way would we send them away.[34] You're a good man," Goodwill said as he began to walk. "Come with me a little way, and I will show you where you need to go."

"Look straight ahead," Goodwill said, pointing ahead of them. "Do you see that narrow Way? The path was constructed by the patriarchs, the prophets, Christ, and even His apostles. It's as straight as an arrow and the way you must go."

"Did you say that it was straight? Are you sure there are no turns or bends in the road that would cause confusion or perhaps get someone lost?"

"Yes, there are many farther down the path. Some are crooked and some wide, but you'll be able to distinguish the right from the wrong because the right path is straight and narrow."[35]

Then in my dream I saw Christian ask him, "Can you help me get this burden off my back?" for Christian knew it was impossible to do so on his own.

Goodwill gave Christian a slight smile. "As for your burden,

---

34 John 6:37
35 Matt. 7:14

you must bear it until you come to the place of Deliverance. There it will fall off your back all by itself."

Christian was so encouraged that he immediately began to prepare for his journey ahead. Goodwill said, "When you've gone some distance from the gate, you'll come to the house of the Interpreter. Knock on his door, and he will show you many good things."

Christian was eager to get started on the road again, so he wished his new friend farewell.

The House of the Interpreter

Christian continued his journey until he came to the house of the Interpreter. He knocked on the door many times until a man finally came and asked, "Who's there?"

Christian stood up straight and replied, "Hello. In my travels, I was told by a man who was very familiar with this house to come here for help. I would like to speak with the one in charge of the house."

The man called for the master of the house, who, after a little while, came to see Christian and asked him the reason for his visit.

"My name is Christian. I've come from the City of Destruction, and I'm heading to Mount Zion. I was told by Goodwill, at the Wicket Gate, that you could show me many good things to help me on my journey."

"Please come in," Interpreter said, opening the door wide and making a sweeping gesture with his hand. "Yes, I can show you many things that will benefit you." With that, he instructed his servant to light a candle, and he told Christian to follow him.

1st Room – The Portrait of the Preacher

The light from the candle guided their way as the Interpreter led him into a private room, where he ordered his servant to open a door. As the door opened, Christian saw a picture of a very serious man hanging on the wall. His eyes looked up to heaven, and he had the best of books—the Bible—in his hand. The law of truth was written on his lips, and the world was behind him. He stood as if pleading with men, and he had a crown of gold hung over his head.

"I'm not sure I understand what this means," Christian said, staring at the painting.

The Interpreter then began to explain the meaning of the painting. "The man you see in this picture is one in a thousand. He can produce children,[36] labor in birth pains,[37] and nurse them himself when they are born. And do you see his eyes looking to heaven, the Bible in his hands, and the law of truth on his lips?"

Christian nodded, listening intently to the Interpreter's every word.

"This is to show you that his work is to know and expose dark things to sinners, even as you see him standing there

---

[36] 1 Cor. 4:15
[37] Gal. 4:19

pleading with men.

"And where you see the world behind him and the crown that hangs over his head, that's to show you that he despises the things of this world for the love that he has for doing God's work. He will surely receive his reward in glory.

"Now," said the Interpreter, turning his attention back to Christian, "I showed you the picture first because the man in the picture is the only man authorized to be your guide through the difficult places you're going. So pay attention and try to remember what you have seen or else you might meet someone on your journey who pretends to lead you the right way, but in reality, their way leads to death."

2nd Room – The Dusty Room

He then took Christian's hand and led him to a very large parlor full of dust because it was never swept. After looking around, the Interpreter instructed a man with a broom to begin sweeping. As he began to sweep, the dust became so thick that Christian nearly choked. Almost immediately, the Interpreter said to a young and gracious lady standing nearby, "Bring some water and sprinkle the room." She did so, and the parlor was swept and cleaned.

"What does this mean?" Christian asked while coughing and clearing the dust out of his lungs.

The Interpreter answered, "The parlor is the heart of a man that was never declared holy by the sweet grace of the Gospel. The dust is his original sin and inward corruptions that have defiled the whole man. The man with the broom is the law, but the gracious young lady who brought water and sprinkled the room is the Gospel.

"As the man with the broom began to sweep, the dust filled the room; it became more difficult to clean, and you almost choked to death. This is to show how the law, instead of cleansing the heart from sin, revives sin, giving it strength to grow and develop in the soul.[38] You can see that the law can both discover and condemn sin, but it has no power to control it.

---

[38] Rom. 5:20, 7:9; 1 Cor. 15:56

"In contrast, the gracious young lady you saw sprinkle the room with water cleaned it easily. This is to show you that the Gospel comes with sweet and precious influences, cleansing the heart and making it livable. Just as you saw the woman settle the dust by sprinkling the floor with water, this is a picture of sin brought under control and the soul made clean through faith, making the heart fit for the King of Glory to inhabit.[39]

[39] John 15:3, Eph. 5:26, Acts 15:9, Rom. 16:25–26

3rd Room – Passion and Patience

Then in my dream, the Interpreter took Christian by the hand and led him into a little room where there were two children, each sitting in a chair. The name of the older child was Passion and the younger Patience. For some reason, Passion appeared restless, agitated, and discontent, but Patience seemed quite calm and content.

Christian asked, "Why is Passion dissatisfied?"

The Interpreter replied, "The governor of these children wants Passion to wait until the first of the year to receive his inheritance, but Passion would rather have it all given to him now. Patience, however, is willing to wait."

Then I saw someone come to Passion and bring him a bag of treasure, which was poured out at his feet. Passion was so happy that he scooped it up, all the while mocking and laughing at Patience. However, before too long, all his treasure had wasted away, and he had nothing left but rags.

Seeing the puzzled look on Christian's face, the Interpreter explained, "These two children represent the men of this world. Patience represents the men who are willing to wait for their inheritance, but Passion represents the men who want their inheritance now, in this present world. He cannot wait until the next year, that is, until eternity. The proverb 'A bird in the hand is worth two in the bush' is his motto for living, meaning material items are worth more than all the treasures of heaven. But you witnessed how quickly Passion wasted it all away until he had nothing left but rags. This is how it will be with men like Passion at the end of this world."

Christian scratched his head while considering all that he had seen and heard from the Interpreter. "I understand now," he said, "that Patience is the wiser of the two for a couple of reasons: first, because he is willing to wait for his inheritance and, secondly, because he will have the glory of his inheritance when the other has nothing but rags."

"Yes," the Interpreter agreed, "and you can add one more reason to that list too: The inheritance that Patience will receive in the next world will never wear out, but the things of this world are gone in an instant. So you can see that Passion really had no reason to mock Patience because he had his inheritance now since it quickly wasted away. On the other hand, Patience could mock Passion because his inheritance will last for eternity. As it is written, the man who is first must yield to the man who is last because the last will have his time to come. But the man who is last yields to no one, for there is no one to follow.

"For that reason, the one who receives his inheritance now will need to use and spend it, but he who receives his inheritance last has it forever. Just like it was said of the rich man, 'In your lifetime you received your good things, and likewise Lazarus evil things, but now he is comforted, and you are tormented.'"[40]

Christian considered this for a moment. "Then that means it's best to not crave after the things of this world but rather to wait for the treasures of the world to come."

"That's true," the Interpreter said as he reached down for Christian's hand and started walking, leading him away. "The things of this world are temporary, but the things we cannot

---

[40] Luke 16:25

see are eternal.[41] But even though we know this to be true, it's still very difficult. You see, our natural desires for the things of this world are very strong and adamantly opposed to spiritual desires for the world to come. It's like they are close neighbors who will never get along."

[41] 2 Cor. 4:18

4th Room – The Roaring Fire

The Interpreter then led Christian into a place where there was a fire burning in a fireplace. A man stood by it, continually throwing buckets of water on the fire, trying to put it out, but the fire continued to burn higher and hotter!

Christian could feel the inviting heat of the roaring fire. "What does this mean?"

The Interpreter answered, "This fire is the work of grace that's been ignited in the heart. The man trying to extinguish it with water is the devil, but even with all his effort, the fire continues to burn higher and hotter. Let me show you why."

He took Christian behind the wall of the fireplace, where there was a man holding a container of oil and secretively throwing the oil on the fire.

"Who is this man, and what's he doing?" Christian asked.

The Interpreter pointed at the man. "This is Christ, who, with the oil of grace, continually maintains the work already begun in the heart.[42] The grace He supplies ignites the soul of His people like a roaring fire that, despite the devil's best efforts, will never be extinguished. This is a difficult concept for man to understand—that even when we are tempted, Christ is doing all the work by supplying the grace we need to stand firm."

---

[42] 2 Cor. 12:9

5th Room – The Palace

Next the Interpreter took Christian to a peaceful place where there was a beautiful and majestic palace. He was captivated by everything he saw, particularly with the sight of several people walking around the top of the palace, clothed in gold.

Christian looked at the pleasant surroundings and the stately and beautiful palace and was enthralled. "Can we go to the palace?"

The Interpreter led him toward the palace door, where a large group of restless, hesitant men were all standing around wanting to enter, but none had the courage.

A little distance from the door sat a man at a table with a book and a pen whose job it was to record the names of everyone courageous enough to enter the palace. Christian then noticed a garrison of fierce, unholy men all dressed in armor guarding the doorway. They were determined not to let anyone pass by them into the palace without a fight to the death. Christian anxiously watched to see what would happen next.

As it happened, the large group of men, who all wanted to enter but lacked courage, began to leave for fear of the armed guards, that is, all but one. Out of the corner of his eye, Christian spotted a valiant man striding up to the man at the table and confidently say, "Sir, write down my name."

As soon as his name was recorded, Christian saw the man draw a sword, put on his helmet, and rush toward the door. The armed men were ready for him, but no amount of deadly force could drive him back. He valiantly cut and hacked through his opponents, delivering more wounds than he received, until eventually he gained entrance into the palace.[43]

Immediately, there heralded a chorus of joy from those inside the palace as well as those walking on top, saying, "Come in! Come in! Eternal glory you shall win!"

So, he went in and was dressed in clothes similar to the ones worn by those in the palace.

Christian, with a confident smile, turned to Interpreter and said, "I think I know the meaning of this. Now let me go in!"

The Interpreter placed his hand on Christian's shoulder, shook his head, and said, "Not just yet. I need you to stay until I show you a little more, and then, after that, you can go your way."

---

[43] Matt. 11:12, Acts 14:22

6th Room – The Caged Man

After this, he took Christian into a dark room, where a man sat in a locked iron cage. The man looked sad and stared down at the ground with his hands folded together. He sighed as if his heart were breaking.

Christian felt sympathy for the man and asked the Interpreter, "What's wrong with him?"

"Why don't you ask him?" responded the Interpreter.

Christian hesitantly approached the man and asked, "What are you doing here?"

The man looked blankly at Christian. "I am now what I once was not."

"What were you once?"

"I once was an active and successful professing Christian, both in my eyes and the eyes of others.[44] At one time, I was totally convinced that I was destined for the Celestial City. In fact, I thought about it all the time and about how happy I would be arriving there."

"I see," Christian said, now even more curious. "But what are you now?"

The man slowly looked back down at the ground. "I'm now a man of captivity, depressed and miserable in this iron cage!"

---

[44] Luke 8:13

Christian began to plead with the man. "Tell me what happened. Why are you in this cage and in this condition?"

"I neglected to watch and be on guard. As a result, I stopped controlling my lust, and now it runs free; I sinned against the truth and goodness of God's Word; I grieved the Holy Spirit, and now He's gone; I flirted with temptation, and the devil came to me; I provoked God to anger, and He abandoned me. At last, I've hardened my heart to the point that I cannot repent."

Christian turned to the Interpreter. "Is there no hope at all for this man?"

"Ask him," said the Interpreter with a nod toward the caged man.

"Don't you have any hope that you'll become free from this cage of despair?"

"No, none. None at all," the man said resolutely.

"But why?" Christian argued. "Are you not aware that the Son of the Blessed is very merciful and gracious?"

"I crucify him daily by how I live.[45] I have despised His person.[46] I have despised His righteousness and regarded His blood as an unholy thing. I have insulted the Spirit of grace[47] and, as a result, shut myself out of all the promises of God. Now the only thing that remains for me is nothing but threats, dreadful threats, and truthful threats of certain judgment and fiery indignation, which will devour me as an enemy."

"Why would you ever let yourself come into this pitiful state?"

"For the lure of the lust, pleasures, and profits of this world," the man said, looking up at Christian again. "I was

---

45 Heb. 6:6
46 Luke 19:14
47 Heb. 10:29

confident that the enjoyment of those things would bring me the happiness I desired, but now every one of those things bites and gnaws at my soul like a burning worm."

"But can't you repent and turn from this terrible way of living?"

"No. God has denied me repentance," the man said, looking back down and shaking his head. "His Word gives me no encouragement to believe. It was He who shut me up in this iron cage, where no man in the world can let me out. Oh, eternity! Eternity! How will I ever wrestle with the misery that I will meet with in eternity?"

"Remember this man's misery," the Interpreter said to Christian, "and let his sorry condition be a warning to you."

"Well, this is very disturbing! I pray that God will make me more aware of the traps that led to this man's misery if it should ever come my way. But, sir," Christian said, extremely eager to leave the caged man behind, "should I not be on my way now?"

"Wait a little longer. I want to show you one more thing before you go."

7th Room – The Unprepared Dreamer

On the last stop, the Interpreter took Christian to a bedroom where a man was getting out of bed. As he put on his clothes, he shook and trembled.

Christian asked, "Why is this man trembling so much?"

The Interpreter instructed the man to explain why he was trembling.

The man could not stop shaking but replied, "This evening, while sleeping, I dreamed the heavens grew extremely black, followed by loud thunder and fierce lightning, which made me very nervous. I looked up in the sky and saw the clouds violently rolling by, followed by a great trumpet sound. Then I saw a Man sitting on a cloud being served by thousands of angels surrounded by a flaming fire that extended to the whole heaven."

The man paused for a moment, took a deep breath, and continued, "I heard a voice call out, saying, 'Arise you who are dead and come to judgment.' Then stones began to shatter, graves were opened, and the dead came to life. Some of the dead were very happy and looked upward, while others tried to hide under the mountains.

"The Man sitting on the cloud opened a book and invited the world to come near. But the fierce flame that surrounded Him kept people at a safe distance, as between a judge and a prisoner on trial.[48]

"The Man then proclaimed to His angels, 'Get together the tares, the chaff, and stubble, and throw them into the burning lake.'[49] And with that the bottomless pit opened, just about where I was standing! Out of its pit spewed forth great billows of smoke and coals of fire, along with hideous noises. Then He said to His angels, 'Gather my wheat into the storehouse.'[50] And with that, I saw many souls caught up and carried away into the clouds, but I was left behind still standing there."[51]

The man was still visibly shaken and could barely get out the next words. "I tried to hide myself, but it was no use, because He kept his eye steady on me. Then all my sins suddenly flooded my mind and accused me on every side.[52] Then I woke up!"

Christian began to tremble himself knowing the answer to his next question even before he asked it. "What was it about all of this that scared you?"

"Why," the man laughed nervously, "I thought the day of judgment had come and that I was not ready for it! But do you want to know the worst of it? It was that the angels gathered up several people near me and left me behind. Then the pit of Hell opened its mouth just where I stood! But the Judge continually kept his eyes focused on me with a look of anger and disapproval while my conscience weighed me down."

Then the Interpreter interrupted and asked Christian, "What do you think about all of these things?"

---

[48] 1 Cor. 15; 1 Thess. 4:16; Jude 15; John 5:28–29; 2 Thess. 1:8–10; Rev. 20:11–14; Isa. 26:21; Micah 7:16–17; Ps. 5:4, 50:1–3; Mal. 3:2–3; Dan. 7:9–10

[49] Matt. 3:12, 18:30, 24:30; Mal. 4:1

[50] Luke 3:17

[51] 1 Thess. 4:16–17

[52] Romans 2:14–15

"They cause me to both hope and fear!"

"Then keep thinking about everything you have seen so that it will drive you forward in the right direction."

As Christian began to prepare himself for his journey the Interpreter said, "I pray the Comforter will always be with you, good Christian, to guide you in the way that leads to the Celestial City."

Before Christian left, he thanked the Interpreter. "You have shown me things rare and profitable, things pleasant and dreadful, things to help me. I will remember these things and begin to understand why they were shown to me."

Chapter Three

Arrival at the Cross

N ow in my dream, I saw Christian on a highway that was fenced on both sides by a wall named Salvation.[53] He started running up the Way but quickly found this difficult due to the burden that was still on his back.

As he ran to the top of what seemed like a small hill, he saw a cross and, below it, a tomb. Just as he approached the cross, his burden fell off his back and tumbled down the hill until it rolled into the opening of the tomb and was never seen again.

Sensing an enormous relief from his burden, Christian became so excited that he cried out in joy, "Jesus has given me rest by means of His sorrow and life by means of His death!"

He stood there for quite a while, weeping as tears streamed down his cheeks.[54] He was in awe of what had just happened. To think that just the sight of the cross could remove his burden and give him peace!

Suddenly three shining angels appeared to him, and one of them said, "Peace be with you! Your sins are forgiven!"[55]

A second angel stripped him of the old rags he was wearing

---

[53] Isa. 26:1
[54] Zech. 12:10
[55] Mark 2:5

and dressed him in new clothes.[56] The third angel placed a mark on his forehead[57] and gave him a certificate with a seal on it. The angel then instructed Christian to look at it for comfort as he ran on the highway and then to deliver it at the gate of the Celestial City. After this, the angels left him.

Christian could barely contain his joy and began leaping while passionately singing:

> *I've traveled so far with my burden of sin,*
> *But no one could ease the grief I was in,*
> *Until I came here! What a place this is!*
> *Is this where I will start being blessed?*
> *Is this where the burden fell off my back?*
> *Is this where the cords that bound it to me broke?*
> *Bless the cross! Bless the tomb! Blessed rather be*
> *The Man who was there put to shame for me!*

---

[56] Zech. 3:4
[57] Eph. 1:13

Simple, Lazy, and Arrogance

Christian continued joyfully on the Way until he came to the bottom of a hill where he saw three men fast asleep with chains attached at their ankles. The name of one was Simple, another was named Lazy, and the third was called Arrogance.

They were all lying around on the ground, and Christian, still full of joy, believed he could help by waking them from their stupor.

"Wake up!" he said. "You're acting like men who are close to drowning in deep waters but completely unaware of the danger you're in. If you'll trust me, I'll help you get these chains off."

Christian was surprised when they did not immediately respond. He tried once again with a more direct approach, saying, "If a roaring lion should come by this way, you will certainly become his prey!"[58]

Completely unconcerned for their welfare, the men merely glanced up at Christian. "I don't see any danger," replied Simple, barely batting an eye at his surroundings before drifting back off to sleep.

Lazy, unwilling to even lift his head, uttered, "I believe a little more sleep will help," as he drifted back off.

---

[58] 1 Peter 5:8

And Arrogance boldly asserted, "Let each man look after himself." And so the three of them lay back down and fell asleep. Christian, knowing there was nothing else he could do, went on his way.

But it troubled him to think that these men, who were in chains and obvious danger, could completely disregard the kindness of another offering to freely help them.

An Encounter with Formalism and Hypocrisy

Christian could not stop thinking about this disturbing encounter as he walked along the Way. Then he spotted two men climbing over the wall on the left-hand side of the narrow Way. Their names were Formalism and Hypocrisy, and they hurried along to catch up with him.

"Gentlemen, where did you come from, and where are you heading?" Christian asked, a little surprised to see them.

Formalism and Hypocrisy replied, "We were born in the land of Vain-glory and are going to Mount Zion to receive praise and honor."

Christian had seen them climbing over the wall and said, "I'm curious. Why did you not enter at the Wicket Gate located at the beginning of the Way? Don't you know that it's written, 'If someone does not enter in the door, but climbs over some other way, that person is the same as a thief and a robber'?"[59]

"That may be true," they said. "However, our countrymen have all agreed that this entrance, or Wicket Gate as you call it, is unnecessary and just too far away. We prefer to take this shortcut right here by climbing over the wall. It's easier and requires less effort."

Christian paused for a moment and then said, "But will the

---

[59] John 10:1

Lord of the Celestial City where we're heading not consider this a violation against His revealed will? Is it not trespassing?"

Formalism and Hypocrisy glanced at each other and smiled. "There's no need to trouble yourself with this. You see, our manner of climbing over this wall has been a long-established tradition. In fact, many witnesses would testify that it's been accepted as an established route for over a thousand years!"

"I understand that this is your tradition," Christian said, "but are you quite sure that your custom will stand up in a court of law?"

"Of course! We don't doubt it for a moment," they said. "An impartial judge would never consider a practice that's been customary for over a thousand years illegal, and besides, what difference does it make how we get on the Way as long as we get on it? If we are in, we are in. As we see it, you arrived on the Way by coming in at the Wicket Gate; we came in by climbing over the wall. What makes your way any better than ours?"

"I will tell you exactly what," Christian said, and he began to explain. "I walk by the rule of my Master, but you walk by the rude workings of your own desires. I have no doubt that the Lord will surely declare you deceitful thieves when you arrive at the end of the Way. You came in by yourselves without His direction, and you will go out by yourselves without His mercy."

The men did not respond to Christian, other than to tell him to mind his own business. All the men continued traveling on the Way without talking, that is, until Formalism and Hypocrisy felt compelled to defend themselves as to the laws and ordinances.

Knowing they were not as conscientious in obeying them as Christian, they said, "We don't see where you're really any different from us except for the coat you're wearing, which was probably given to you by one of your neighbors to cover the shame of your nakedness."

Christian was struck by their directness and said, "I would not be counting on laws and ordinances to save you since you did not come in by the Wicket Gate.[60] And as for the coat I'm wearing, it was given to me by the Lord of the Celestial City, as you say, to cover my nakedness. I consider it a token of His kindness to me since I previously had nothing but rags. Besides, it brings me comfort as I travel on the Way. I have no doubt that when I arrive at the gate of the Celestial City, the Lord will know me since I'm wearing the coat that He freely gave me on the day He stripped me of my rags.

"And what's more, perhaps you have noticed this mark on my forehead. It was placed there by one of His shining angels the day my burden fell off my back. In addition to all of this, I was given this sealed certificate to read for comfort as I go along the Way. I was told to return it once I arrived at the gate of the Celestial City as a token of my authorization to enter. However, I doubt that you're concerned about any of these things since you did not enter at the Wicket Gate."

Once again, they had no answer for Christian. Instead, they looked at each other and burst out laughing. Christian decided there was no need to continue this journey anymore with them, so he moved on ahead. Sometimes he would talk to himself, other times he would groan, while still many other times he would feel refreshed from reading the certificate that the angel had given him.

---

[60] Gal. 2:16

Climbing the Hill of Difficulty

They all continued traveling on the Way until arriving at the foot of the Hill of Difficulty, where there was a spring. There was also an intersection of two other ways that came straight from the Wicket Gate, one that turned to the left and one to the right of the hill, but the narrow Way that Christian was told to take went straight up the hill called Difficulty.

Christian was thirsty, so he walked over and drank from the Spring of Life.[61] He then went straight up the hill, saying, "Regardless of how high and difficult this hill is, I'm determined to walk up it because I know it leads to the Way of Life. I might become weak or even scared, but I will have courage and press on because it's better to be on the right path, even if it's difficult, than to go an easier way that ends in misery."

When Formalism and Hypocrisy came to the foot of the hill, they stopped in their tracks when they saw how steep and high the narrow Way was. It was then they noticed the two alternative roads, one to the right and the other to the left of the hill. After talking it over, they assumed these would be easier routes and would likely meet up with Christian on the other side. The name of one of these roads was Danger and the other Destruction. One turned to the left on the way of Danger

---

[61] Isa. 49:10

and lost his way in a great forest. The other took the right on the way to Destruction, which led him to a wide field full of dark mountains, where he stumbled and fell, never to be seen again.

I then looked back at Christian to see how far he had made it up the hill. At first I saw him run, then walk, and then resort to crawling on his hands and knees because of how steep it was.

Now, about halfway to the top, there was a shady arbor made by the Lord of the hill for those who traveled by that they might find rest. Exhausted, Christian sat down, took the certificate out of his chest pocket, and began to read it for comfort. He also stopped and was pleased to admire his new clothes given to him when he stood before the cross.

After reading the certificate and feeling quite content, he nodded off into a deep sleep, dropping the certificate from his hand.

Around sunset, someone approached and shook Christian awake, saying, "You lazy fool, look at the ant and watch it closely; let it teach you a thing or two."[62] At this, Christian jumped up and started on his way, trying to make up for lost time. He raced ahead until he came to the top of the hill.

---

[62] Prov. 6:6

The Fear of Nervousness and Mistrust

When he was close to the top of the hill, two men, named Nervousness and Mistrust, came running down at full force to meet him. Christian held up his hands to slow them down. "What's the matter?" he said. "Don't you realize that you're running the wrong way?"

"We were going to the City of Zion," said Nervousness, pointing up the hill, "but the farther we climbed up the Hill of Difficulty, the more danger we encountered! It just became too risky, so we got scared and decided to turn around and head back home."

"Not only that," said Mistrust, trying to catch his breath, "but we came upon two lions lying in the Way in front of us! We weren't sure if they were asleep or not, but we knew they would attack us if we got too close and tear us limb from limb!"

Christian began to feel a little uneasy. "Now you have me fearing what's ahead! But where else can I go to be safe? If I go back home to the City of Destruction, which is destined for fire and brimstone, I will die there for sure. However, I know I will be safe if I can just make it to the Celestial City.

"It seems to me that if I turn back now, I will certainly die. If I go forward, I might experience the fear of death but with the assurance of everlasting life." With that, Christian knew what he must do. "There's no question—I must move forward!"

Mistrust and Nervousness just shook their heads and ran down the hill while Christian continued traveling on the difficult Way.

As he walked, Christian could not stop thinking about the frightening story the men had told. For comfort, he reached down to his chest pocket to feel for his certificate, but to his surprise, it was not there! He immediately began to panic, not knowing what to do. The certificate was not only there to relieve him of his fears but also to provide him entrance into the Celestial City.

Then he recalled sleeping in the shady arbor by the side of the hill and suspected that he had lost the certificate there. Feeling like a lazy fool, he fell to his knees and prayed that God would forgive him. He then got up and raced back down the hill to find it. With each step, Christian's heart grew heavier and heavier. Sometimes he sighed, other times he wept, and often he just scolded himself, saying, "I'm such a fool for sleeping during the day in a place meant only to provide temporary rest."

Farther and farther he ran back down the hill, carefully retracing each step, looking all around for any sight of the certificate that had provided him so much comfort. As the shady arbor came into view, where he had rested and slept, he was once again filled with remorse for what he had done.[63]

"I'm such a miserable person that I should sleep in the daytime!" he bemoaned. "In the middle of difficulty, I should so indulge myself by sleeping in a place that the Lord of the Hill provided only for the temporary relief of weary travelers!"

"How many needless steps have I taken with no result? This is exactly what happened to Israel. They were sent back again to wander in the wilderness by way of the Red Sea because of

---

[63] Rev. 2:4, 1 Thess. 5:6–8

their sin. In the same way, I'm forced to walk this way again in misery that might have been walked in joy had it not been for this sinful sleep. I know I would have been so much farther on my journey by this time! Instead, I must walk these steps three times instead of once. And now it's starting to get dark, and the day is almost over. I wish I had never slept!"

Reaching the arbor, he sat down and wept. Then, looking around, he spotted his certificate under the seat! He was so excited that he quickly grabbed the certificate and thrust it into his chest pocket.

Christian's spirit erupted with cries of joyful praise to God for the certificate was his assurance of salvation and acceptance at the Celestial City. He pressed the certificate to his heart and gave thanks to God for directing his eyes to where it was lying. With joyful tears, he focused on moving ahead in his journey.

Oh, how carefully did he climb the rest of the hill! But as he reached the top, Christian noticed the sun was going down. He painfully recalled the foolishness of his sleeping and how it had delayed him from being so much farther ahead by now. In his grief, he said, "My sinful sleep has caused me so much difficulty! Because of it, my journey, which should have been during the daylight, is now in the darkness of night! I must now walk in the dark, not knowing where to step next, all while hearing the noises of frightening creatures, just because of my miserable sleep."

Then he remembered the story of Mistrust and Nervousness and how scared they were at the sight of lions in the path. Christian thought to himself, *These beasts prowl in the night, seeking their prey, so if they should meet me in the dark, how will I avoid being torn to pieces?*

He cautiously went on his way, complaining about his terrible circumstances. Then, he looked up and saw a magnificent palace directly in front of him, called the Palace Beautiful. It stood to one side of the Way.

Chapter 4

Arrival at the Palace Beautiful

In my dream, I saw Christian hurry along the path toward the palace, hoping that he might find lodging there for a while. Before he had gone far, he entered onto a very narrow path about two hundred twenty yards from the palace lodge.

As the path continued to narrow, he spotted the same two lions that had frightened Mistrust and Nervousness and sent them running back home. The lions were ferocious and seemed as though they might maul him to death if he got too close. Christian was terrified and began to think of turning around and going home too. (What Christian could not see was the chain that was restraining the wild beasts.)

The porter at the palace lodge, whose name was Watchman, noticed Christian was thinking of retreating, so he cried out to him, "Is your strength and courage so small?[64] Don't be afraid of the lions, because they are chained. They are placed there on your journey as a trial of faith and to reveal those that have no faith. Just stay in the middle of the Way, and you will not be harmed."

Christian was quite scared but went forward anyway, being careful to follow the Watchman's instructions. The lions

---

[64] Mark 4:40

roared and snarled, but they did not hurt him as he stayed in the middle of the Way. Finally, he made it to the gate, where Watchman was waiting for him, and he clapped his hands with joy!

Feeling both confident and relieved, Christian turned to Watchman and asked, "Sir, whose residence is this, and may I stay here tonight?"

"This palace was built by the Lord of the Hill for those that are traveling to find safety and rest," said Watchman, eyeing Christian closely. "Tell me, where did you come from, and where are you going?"

"I'm from the City of Destruction and heading to Mount Zion," Christian said, "but now the sun has gone down, and if you would allow me, I would like to stay here tonight."

"What's your name?"

"My name is Christian, but it used to be Graceless. I come from the family of Japheth, whom God will persuade to dwell in the tents of Shem."[65]

With a concerned look, Watchman asked, "But why are you coming here so late after the sun has set?"

Christian looking down in shame said, "I would have been here much sooner, but because of the wretched man that I am, I fell asleep in the shady arbor located on the side of the Hill of Difficulty! If it were not for that and then losing my certificate while I slept there, I would not have been late. Unfortunately, I realized that it was lost once I arrived at the top of the hill. Without hesitation, I ran back and found it then pressed forward on my journey, arriving here late."

"Well, I will talk to one of the maidens of this place," said Watchman. "If she likes what you have to say, she will invite you to join the rest of the family, according to the rules of the

---

[65] Gen. 9:27

house."

Then Watchman rang a bell. A beautiful and dignified maiden named Discretion came to the door of the house and asked, "Why did you call me?"

Watchman responded, "This man is on a journey from the City of Destruction to Mount Zion. Now the sun has set, and he is weary and tired and has asked if he might stay here tonight. I told him I would call for you and you would, after some discussion with him, decide what seemed best according to the rules of the house."

Discretion asked Christian where he came from and where he was going, and he told her. She asked him how he got on the path, so he told her. Then she asked him what he had seen and met with on the path, and he told her that too.

Finally, she asked him his name. "My name is Christian," he said. "I really would like to stay here tonight because I understand that this place was built by the Lord of the Hill for the safety and rest of pilgrims."

As she smiled, tears came to her eyes. After a slight pause, she said, "I will call for two or three more of the family to come here." She ran to the door and called to Prudence, Piety, and Charity, who came out to meet him. After talking with him a little more, they brought him inside to meet the rest of the family.

Many of them came and warmly welcomed Christian as he entered the house, saying, "Come in! You are blessed of the Lord! This house was built by the Lord of the Hill for the express purpose of entertaining pilgrims like you."

Christian bowed his head and followed them into the palace. Once inside, he sat down and was given something to drink. To make the best use of time, they all agreed that until supper was ready, a few of them would continue talking with Christian, namely, Piety, Prudence, and Charity.

An Interview with Piety, Prudence, and Charity

"Come with us, Christian," Piety said, leading the way into another room, where they all sat down. "Since we have shown you love and hospitality by inviting you into our house tonight, we think it would be good for you to share your story with us about all the things that have happened on your journey."

"I would be happy to!" Christian said, excited about the opportunity to share his experience. "Thank you for allowing me to stay here."

Piety smiled and began with her first question. "What first made you decide to follow this way of life?"

Christian leaned back in his chair and thought for a moment. "I was driven out of my own country by a terrible message that I kept hearing telling me that I would die if I stayed in the City of Destruction."

"Well, what finally happened to make you leave your country and head this way?" she asked.

"God had a plan," he said. "You see, I was overwhelmed with the fear of death and didn't know which way to go, but by chance, a man named Evangelist found me while I was shaking and crying and directed me to the Wicket Gate. Otherwise, I would have never found it. He also set me on the Way that led directly to this house."

Piety's brow furrowed as she seemed confused by the

answer. "But didn't you also pass by the House of the Interpreter?"

"Oh yes!" Christian said with a big smile stretching across his face. "That's an experience I will remember for as long as I live. I saw many incredible things there, but there were three things that impacted me most. The first was to understand how Christ, in opposition to Satan, maintains His work of grace in the heart. The second was how the man in the iron cage had sinned himself into such despair that he had no hope of God's mercy. The third was the dream of the man who had imagined that the day of judgment had come, and he was not prepared."

"Did you hear him tell his dream?"

"Yes," Christian said with a serious look. "It was a terrible discovery. My heart hurt just to hear him tell it. But I'm glad I did."

"Was this *all* you saw at the House of the Interpreter?"

"No," Christian said, shaking his head. "He showed me a stately palace filled with people dressed in gold. Then a courageous man came forward and cut his way through the armed men who stood in the door of the palace to keep him out. Once the man got through, he was invited to come into the palace and receive eternal glory. My heart and mind were completely overwhelmed by what I saw. In fact, I would have stayed at the Interpreter's house for a year, but I knew that I had some distance to go."

Piety paused for a moment and then leaned in closer to Christian and asked, "What *else* did you see on the way?"

"What *else* did I see?" Christian was obviously more excited as he moved to the edge of seat. "Well, I had no more traveled a little farther down the path when I saw, as if it were in my mind, a Man hanging on a tree bleeding. Just the very sight of Him made the burden fall off my back, and this was a great burden that I had been suffering with for some time. It was unbelievable! It just fell off my back. It surprised me because I'd never seen such a thing before!

"While I stood staring at the cross, almost in a daze, three shining angels appeared before me. One declared my sins forgiven. Another stripped me of my rags and gave me the new embroidered coat that I'm wearing. The third angel placed the mark that you see on my forehead and gave me this sealed certificate." He pulled the certificate from his chest pocket and showed it to her.

Piety leaned back in her chair. "I'm guessing you saw even more than this on the Way, didn't you?"

Nodding his head, Christian said, "What I've told you is the very best, but yes, I did see many interesting things. For instance, I saw three men, Simple, Lazy, and Arrogance, lying asleep a little off the Way with chains on their ankles. It was nearly impossible to wake them!

"I also saw Formality and Hypocrisy come tumbling over the wall and pretending to go to Mount Zion. But they were quickly lost. Even though I had warned them, they simply would not believe.

"I did, however, work very hard to get up this hill and became quite stressed about the thought of lions devouring me. I'll tell you the truth. Had it not been for the good porter standing at the gate, I might have gone back home again. Praise God I'm here, and thank you for welcoming me."

Then Prudence, quite eager to join the conversation, said, "Do you sometimes think about the City of Destruction?"

"Yes," he said, slowly leaning back in his chair again, "but only with shame and disgust. Truth be told, if I had a deep longing to return to that country, I probably would have done so by now. But my heart desires a better country, that is, a heavenly one.[66] So I will press on."

"Even now, do you still think about your old life and the people you were involved with?"

Christian knew that he did and was ashamed to say it. "Yes, those thoughts do enter my mind but greatly against my will, especially regarding my physical thoughts and desires. You see, where I come from, physical desires consume our minds, and we love to think about them. But now all those thoughts and memories bring nothing but grief. If I could choose what entered my mind, I would never choose to think of those things again. But even on my best days, the worst of those thoughts still remain in me."[67]

"Do you find yourself sometimes able to overcome certain thoughts while at other times find it much more difficult?" asked Prudence.

"Yes, but not that often, although when they do occur, those times are truly golden."

Not completely satisfied with the answer, Prudence kept digging. "When you experience those times of overcoming your physical desires, are you aware how you defeated them?"

"Oh, absolutely!" Christian said, nodding. "When I think about what I saw at the cross, that will do it. When I look upon my embroidered coat, that will do it. When I look at the certificate that I carry in my chest pocket, that will do it. And when I think about going to the Celestial City, that will do it."

Prudence pressed further. "And why do you so desire to go to the Celestial City?"

Without hesitation and with a gleam in his eye, Christian shouted and almost jumped out of his seat. "Why, it's there that I hope to see Him alive who was hanging dead on the

---

[66] Heb. 11:15–16
[67] Rom. 7:15–21

cross! It's there that I hope to get rid of all those things that to this day remain a constant annoyance. For in the Celestial City, they say there is no death and that I will be living with the best of heavenly companions. But most of all, I love Him because He released me from my burden, and I'm so tired of being sick inside. I would prefer to be where I will die no more and with my companions who will continually cry, "Holy, Holy, Holy!"[68]

Charity jumped into the conversation. "Do you have a family, Christian? Are you married?"

The excitement that was on Christian's face suddenly started to fade as he fell back into his chair. "I have a wife and four small children."

Looking around, she asked, "And why did you not bring them along with you?"

The thought of his family made him break down and weep. "Oh, how I wanted to! But they were adamantly opposed to going on this journey with me."

"You should have talked to them and tried to show them the danger of staying behind," Charity said.

"I did!" he cried. "I showed them exactly what God had revealed to me about the coming destruction of our city, but they just laughed and did not believe me."[69]

"Did you also pray that God would help them understand your warning?" she asked.

"Yes. I prayed so passionately for them. You must understand," Christian said, thinking only of his wife and children, "I love my family very much."

"Did you also share with them your own feelings of stress and fear of the coming destruction? I'm sure the prospect of

---

[68] Isa. 25:8, Rev. 21:4
[69] Gen. 19:14

destruction was clear enough to you."

Christian placed his head in his hands and leaned forward on his knees. "Oh yes, again, again, and again. I was unable to hide the fear on my face or the tears in my eyes when I thought about the judgment coming for us all. But none of it was sufficient to convince them to come with me."

"But what reason did they give for not coming along?" she asked.

Christian slowly lifted his head up and wiped away some tears. "Well, for one, my wife was afraid of losing all the comforts and attractions of this world. And as for my children, they are completely absorbed with the foolish pleasures of youth. For one reason or another, they left me to wander, anxiously thinking about our fate."

Charity paused to allow Christian to compose himself. "So with all your effort to persuade your family to come with you and leave the City of Destruction, do you think it was your new way of life that discouraged them from following you?"

Christian held up his hand and shook his head. "No, I cannot and will not commend my own life. I'm well aware of my many personal failings. I also know that by living a hypocritical life, a man can quickly undo whatever argument or persuasion he has used to present the good news. But I can say that I was very careful to avoid any disgraceful behavior that would give them reason to avoid going on this journey with me.

"In fact, if anything, I was too strict and denied myself things, for their sake, in which they saw nothing wrong. I can honestly say that if what they saw in me hindered them, it was my great caution in not wanting to sin against God or others."

"Undoubtedly so," Charity said, nodding as if understanding Christian's plight. "Cain hated his brother because his own works were evil and his brother's righteous.[70] If your wife and children have been offended by this, then they show themselves unyielding toward that which is good. You have delivered your soul from accountability for their blood."[71]

---

[70] 1 John 3:12
[71] Ezek. 3:19

Suiting Up for Battle

They continued talking until supper was ready then all sat down to eat around a table furnished with the most delicious and rich foods and the best wine. All the talk at the table was on the Lord of the Hill, specifically, what He had done, why He did it, and why He built the Palace. From what they said, Christian understood that He had been a great warrior and fought with and slain the one who had the power over death but not without great danger to Himself, which made Christian love Him even more.

"For as I understand and believe," said Christian, referring to the great warrior, "He was victorious but not without losing a lot of blood. But He did it all for the glory of grace and with a motive of pure love for His people."[72]

At the table, there were other residents of the house who claimed to have seen and talked with Him since His death on the cross. They testified to having heard from His own lips that He loves poor pilgrims more than the east is from the west.

They said that at another time He stripped Himself of His glory for the poor, and they also heard Him say that He would not live in Mount Zion alone. Furthermore, He had made many pilgrims into princes, who by their own very nature were born repulsive beggars.[73]

---

[72] Heb. 2:14–15
[73] 1 Sam. 2:8, Ps. 113:7

They continued talking until late in the evening, at which time they committed themselves to the Lord for protection and each went to their own bed. Christian was provided a large upstairs bedroom with a window that opened toward the east to catch the sunrise. The bedroom was named Peace.

On waking the next morning, he joyfully sang,

"Where am I now? Is this the love and care of Jesus?
For the men that pilgrims are,
To provide that I should be forgiven?
And live already the next door to heaven!"

That morning they all got up and continued talking, but as Christian was preparing to leave, they asked him to stay and see the variety of rare treasures and relics in the house. First, they took him into the study, where they showed him records of the greatest age, which included the recorded ancestry of the Lord of the Hill. It proved that He was the Son of the Ancient of Days and came from an eternal generation. These records also revealed the acts that He had accomplished and the names of hundreds of people that He had recruited into His service. They also showed how He had placed them in such living conditions that would never decay or dissolve with the passing of time.

Then they read to him some of the notable acts that some of his servants had done, including how they had subdued kingdoms, brought about righteousness, obtained promises, stopped the mouths of lions, quenched the violence of fire, and escaped the edge of the sword. Out of their weakness, they were made strong and became courageous in battle, which made foreign enemies flee.[74]

---

[74] Heb. 11:33-34

They read another part of the house record that revealed how willing their Lord was to receive any person into His good graces. This included those that had previously insulted His character and accomplishments.

Here Christian also viewed a variety of historical documents concerning other famous events, both ancient and modern. He saw prophecies and predictions of things guaranteed to be fulfilled, both to the dread and amazement of enemies and the comfort and relief of His pilgrims.

The next day they led him into the armory, where they showed him all kinds of military weapons that their Lord had specifically provided to pilgrims for battle. There was a sword, shield, helmet, breastplate, all-prayer, and shoes that would not wear out. There was enough here to outfit as many men for the service of their Lord as there were stars in the heavens.

They also showed him some of the military equipment that many of His warriors had used to accomplish wonderful things. This included the rod of Moses; the hammer and nail with which Jael had killed Sisera; the pitchers, trumpets, and lamps that Gideon used to defeat the Midianites; and the ox goad Shamgar used to kill six hundred men. They also brought out the jaw bone of an ass that Samson had used to accomplish such great feats. Moreover, they showed him the sling and stone David had used to kill Goliath of Gath and the sword that their Lord would use to eventually kill the man of sin and have final victory over the predator. Christian was delighted to view all of this and did so until late in the evening, at which time they all went to bed.

On the next day, as Christian was preparing to leave again, they said, "Please stay here just one more day. We would like to show you the Delectable Mountains, which we believe will provide you comfort the closer you get to the Celestial City."

Christian agreed to stay, and the next morning they brought him up to an observation point on the roof of the palace and said, "Look to the south." When he did, he clearly saw a beautiful land full of hills, woods, vineyards, fruits of all sorts, and flowers, with streams and fountains. It was an amazing sight to behold![75]

Christian was awestruck and asked, "What is the name of this land?"

"Immanuel's Land," they said. "This land is designed for you, and others like you, and is like the Palace on this hill. When you reach the land, you'll have a great view of the gate of the Celestial City, which the shepherds who live there will show you."

Everyone agreed it was now time for Christian to depart. "But before you go," they said, "let's return to the armory."

In the armory, they equipped Christian from head to toe with fully tested weapons in case he should encounter assaults along the way. Once fully outfitted, he walked out with his friends to the Palace gate, where he asked Watchman, "Have you seen any pilgrims pass by?"

"Yes, I have," Watchman replied.

"Tell me, did you know him?"

"I asked his name, and he told me it was Faithful."

"Oh, I know him!" Christian said happily. "He is a neighbor from my hometown and comes from the City of Destruction, where I was born. How far ahead of me do you think he may be?"

Watchman shrugged his shoulders and said, "By this time, he's probably beyond the bottom of the hill."

Christian placed his hand on Watchman's shoulder. "Watchman, you're a good man. May the Lord be with you and bless you abundantly for all of the kindness you have

---

[75] Isa. 33:16–17

shown me."

Then Christian begin to leave, and Discretion, Piety, Charity, and Prudence all agreed to accompany him down to the bottom of the hill. As they walked, they reminded Christian of the truth and promises of the Lord of the Hill, as they had in the palace.

"As difficult as this hill was to come up," said Christian, "it seems even more dangerous going down."

"Yes," said Prudence, "It's a hard thing for a man to go down to the Valley of Humiliation, as you are doing right now, and not slip in any way. This is the reason we have come with you to the bottom of the hill." Even so, Christian walked down very carefully, still stumbling a time or two.

When they all got to the bottom of the hill, Christian's new friends gave him a loaf of bread, a bottle of wine, and a cluster of raisins; then they left him to go on his way.

Christian was grateful for the encouragement that Discretion, Piety, Charity, and Prudence had shared and for their help in relieving him of his grief. When they departed, he was fully clad with northern steel from head to toe.

Chapter Five
The Battle with Apollyon

Christian found it difficult traveling through the Valley of Humiliation. The Way was hard, and he had only gone a short distance when he spotted an evil beast named Apollyon (meaning destroyer) coming across the field to meet him.

The sight of Apollyon filled Christian with fear, and he wondered whether he should turn and run or stand his ground. After considering his options, he realized that if he were to turn and run, he would be easy prey for Apollyon to shoot him with darts since he had no armor for his back. So he decided to go forward and stand his ground, knowing it was the only way to truly save his life. He gripped his sword for comfort and walked forward on the path to meet Apollyon.

Now, the beast was hideous and clothed with scales like a fish (these were his pride). He had wings like a dragon and feet like a bear; out of his belly spewed fire and smoke, and he had the mouth of a lion.

He approached Christian, looking at him in disdain then sharply barked, "Where did you come from, and where are you going?"

Christian cleared his throat and timidly responded, "I came from the evil City of Destruction, and I'm going to the City of Zion."

"Ah...then you're one of my subjects because the City of Destruction is mine. You see, I'm its prince and god." Apollyon's eyes narrowed in on Christian as if he might strike him at any moment. "Why have you run away from your king? If I thought you were unable to provide me any more work, I would strike you to the ground with one blow."

Even though he was scared, Christian stood up straight and bravely said, "Yes, it's true that I was born in your land, but you worked us too hard, and no man could live on your wages, for the wages of sin is death.[76] So when I became of age, I did as any other thoughtful person might do and tried to renew myself."

"No prince likes to lose his subjects, and I do not intend to lose you." An evil smile formed around his lion-shaped mouth, revealing his jagged teeth. "But since you have complained of your work and wages, I personally promise to pay you as much as our land can afford if you will go back."

Christian shook his head and said, "That's not an option. I've already sold myself to the King of princes. In all fairness, how can I go back with you?"

Apollyon's smile disappeared. He gritted his teeth and took a step toward Christian. "It seems to me as though your decisions have gone from bad to worse. But I'm not surprised. Many have professed themselves to this King you mentioned but, after a while, gave Him the slip and returned to me. You will do so too eventually, and all will be well."

Christian was shocked at the assertion that he would abandon his King. "I've professed my faith and sworn my allegiance to Him! How can I go back on this and not be hanged as a traitor?"

Apollyon shrugged his shoulders. "You did the same to me, and yet here I am, willing to let it all go if you will just turn

---

[76] Rom. 6:23

and go back to the City of Destruction."

"Any commitment I made to you was in my youth. I'm confident that the King under whose banner I now stand will both absolve and pardon me for what I did while working for you."

Christian, now feeling a little more confident, took a step forward. "And let me offer some more truth, you who destroy! I like His work, His wages, His servants, His government, His company, and His land much better than yours. Leave me alone and do not try to persuade me anymore. I'm His servant now and will follow Him!"

"Perhaps you should cool down and rethink this path you're on while you still can," Apollyon snarled. "You are aware that for the most part, His servants have come to an early grave because they resisted me and my ways, and many have even been put to shameful deaths!"

Apollyon paused to let what he had said sink in then added, "And besides, why do you think His work is better than mine? He has never come to rescue any of His servants out of their enemies' hands. But as for me, how many times, as all the world very well knows, have I delivered, either by power or fraud, those who have faithfully served me even when they were taken by Him and His followers! And so I will deliver you, Christian."

Christian took another step forward, feeling braver with each step. "You have it all wrong, Apollyon! Any delay on deliverance is on purpose to test their love and to prove whether they will be loyal to Him to the end. And even though you think they came to a deadly end, they were immediately delivered into glory! In this life, they do not expect to be delivered, for they know they will receive their glory when the King comes in His glory with the angels."

This made Apollyon howl in anger as he leveled his bony

finger at Christian. "You have already been unfaithful in your service to Him, so how do you expect to receive wages from Him?"

Christian took yet another step forward, gripping his sword tighter. "Tell me, Apollyon, where have I been unfaithful to Him?"

Apollyon's indignation was evident as he spoke quickly, spewing smoke from his nostrils. "You were unfaithful when you first set out and almost drowned in the Swamp of Despair. You were unfaithful trying to rid yourself of your burden the wrong way when you should have waited for your King to take it off. You were unfaithful when you fell into a sinful sleep and lost the certificate. You were unfaithful when you were almost persuaded to go back at the sight of the lions on the Way."

Apollyon stopped and glared at Christian as if he had him then said in a mocking tone, "And when you talked of your journey and all that you have seen and heard, oh, how you inwardly desired everyone's praise, and your pride was evident for all to see."

Christian nodded in agreement. "Yes, Apollyon. All of this is true and even much more that you have left out. But the King whom I serve and honor is merciful and ready to forgive me."

Taking another step toward the beast he said, "The fact is, I had many weaknesses in your land, mainly because I was brought up, and educated that way. But now that weight has been lifted and I'm sorry for them. Most importantly, I've obtained pardon from my King."

Then Apollyon broke out into a great rage and said, "I hate that King, and I hate His laws and people. I've come out with the sole purpose of standing against you!"

Christian put one hand on his sword and held up the other. "Apollyon, beware what you do, for I'm on the King's highway, the way of holiness. This is your final warning!"

Then Apollyon straddled the entire path in front of Christian, blocking the Way. "I don't fear anything you say," he hissed. "Prepare to die! I swear by my infernal den that you will go no farther. It's here that I will spill your soul."

Without even hesitating, Apollyon shot a flaming dart at his chest! But Christian had the shield in his hand, and with it, he was able to intercept the arrows and avoid danger.

Christian drew his sword quickly, knowing it was time to attack, but Apollyon was quicker and charged at him, shooting darts as thick as hail. Christian did all he could to defend himself and fight back, but Apollyon began to overpower him and inflicted wounds to his head, hand, and foot. This caused Christian to fall back a little, leading Apollyon to follow with another round of forceful attacks.

This severe combat lasted for over half a day. Christian was courageous and fought as bravely as he could, but his wounds were deep and he was exhausted, growing weaker and weaker with each attack.

Then Apollyon, seeing his opportunity, forced himself closer to Christian and, wrestling with him, threw him down with such great force that the sword flew out of Christian's hand.

"I've got you now!" Apollyon screeched with delight as he began to beat him mercilessly so that Christian wished he was dead.

But by the grace of God, while Apollyon was preparing for his fatal blow, Christian quickly reached out his hand, felt for his double-edged sword, and grabbed it. "Don't celebrate just yet, Apollyon, because when I fall, I will rise!"[77]

And with that, Christian thrust his sword into Apollyon,

---

[77] Mic. 7:8

which made the beast fall back as if he was mortally wounded. Seizing his opportunity, Christian swung his sword again, striking the beast and yelling, "Even so, in all these things we are more than conquerors through Him that loved us!"[78] Then Apollyon spread out his dragon wings and quickly sped away until Christian could see him no more.[79]

During this battle, no one can imagine (unless they had seen and heard as I did) what yelling and hideous roaring Apollyon made during the fight, for he spoke as a dragon, and, on the other side of the fight, what sighing and groaning burst from Christian's heart. I never saw Christian give so much as one pleasant look throughout the battle, that is, until he knew he had wounded Apollyon with his double-edged sword. Then, indeed, he smiled and looked upward with thanksgiving! But it was the most dreadful battle I ever saw.

When the battle was over, Christian said, "I'll give thanks in this place to Him who delivered me out of the mouth of the lions—to Him who helped me against Apollyon. Great Beelzebub, the captain of this beast, made plans to ruin me. He did so by sending out Apollyon with hellish rage to engage me in a fierce battle. But thankfully Michael helped me and, by the steel of my sword, made him quickly fly away. Therefore, to Him let me give lasting praise and always be thankful and bless His holy name."

Then a Hand appeared to Christian offering him some of the leaves of the Tree of Life. He took them and applied them to the wounds that he had received in the battle and was healed immediately. He also sat down in that place to eat bread and drink of the bottle that was given to him a little earlier.

Feeling refreshed, he began his journey again with the sword still drawn in his hand. "Who knows if there might be

---

[78] Rom. 8:37
[79] James 4:7

some other enemy at hand." But the remainder of his journey through this valley was quiet, and he was not challenged by Apollyon again.

Entering the Valley of the Shadow of Death

At the end of this valley stretched another called the Valley of the Shadow of Death. This valley was a very lonely and desolate place, but Christian knew that to get to the Celestial City, he must pass through it. The prophet Jeremiah described this valley as "A wilderness, a land of deserts and pits, a land of drought, and of the Shadow of Death, a land that no man (but a Christian) passes through, and where no man lives."[80] It was here Christian was subjected to more hardship than when battling Apollyon, as you will see by what follows.

As he reached the border of the Valley of the Shadow of Death, he came upon two men. They were descendants of the spies who had brought back a bad report of the Promised Land. They were in a hurry to get back home.[81]

Christian stopped them and asked, "Where are you going?"

"We are going back...back to where we came from!" they said, quite flustered and in a hurry. "And quite honestly, we think you should do the same if you value your life and peace of mind."

Christian furrowed his brow. From what he could see looking out across the valley, the land looked rough and somewhat concerning, but perhaps these men were

---

[80] Jer. 2:6
[81] Num. 13:32

overreacting, so he asked, "Why? What's the matter with the Way ahead?"

"What's the matter!" they cried. "We'll tell you what the matter is! We were going the way you are now and went only as far as we dared. In fact, we were almost past the point of no return, and had we gone a little farther, we would not be here to bring you this news!"

Now Christian was starting to get impatient with the two men. "What news? What did you encounter?"

"Why, we were almost in the Valley of the Shadow of Death, but fortunately we looked ahead and realized the danger we were about to get into!"[82]

Christian was almost beside himself with anticipation, so he blurted out, "But what did you see?"

"What did we see?" They glanced around as if someone were watching them and lowered their voices. "Why, we saw the valley itself! It was as dark as pitch, and there were hobgoblins, satyrs, and dragons of the pit. We heard a continual howling and yelling from people experiencing unspeakable misery, writhing in pain, and bound with chains. When you look up, all you see is discouraging clouds of confusion, while death spreads its wings over the entire valley. To sum it up, it's as every bit as dreadful as it sounds, and there's nothing there but disorder."[83]

Christian looked over the bleak and dismal valley. "To tell you the truth, I've never seen anything in my life like what you've just described. But this is the only road to the Celestial City, so I must stay on it."[84]

"It might be your road, but it's not ours anymore!" With that, the two men left. Based on their dire report, Christian

---

[82] Ps. 44:19, 107:19

[83] Job 3:5, 10:22

[84] Ps. 44:18–19, Jer. 2:6

moved forward cautiously, but his sword remained drawn in case he was assaulted.

In my dream, I could see the entire valley. As far as it stretched, there was a very deep ditch on the right-hand side—the same ditch in which the blind have led the blind throughout time and have both perished miserably there. On the left-hand side of the valley, there was a very dangerous quagmire into which if even a good man falls he can find no solid footing to stand. King David once fell into that same quagmire and would have eventually smothered had the Lord not delivered him and pulled him out.[85]

In the middle of the ditch and mire, the Way was extremely narrow, so Christian had to be very careful where he walked. He searched in the dark for any solid ground while trying to avoid falling into the ditch on one side and stumbling into the mire on the other. In the same way, if he overcompensated and tried to escape the mire, unless he was very careful, he would find himself on the brink of falling into the ditch. His heart was racing and he was breathing heavily, for besides the danger he was in, the Way here was so dark that he often could not see where his next step would land.

In the middle of this valley, I could see the very mouth of Hell right next to the narrow Way. When Christian saw it, he wondered what he should do because the flames and smoke were so thick that it seemed to surround him. There were also sparks and hideous screaming and groaning that were not in the least bit intimidated by Christian's sword, as Apollyon had been before. He sheathed his sword and resorted to another weapon called all-prayer.

I heard him cry out, "O Lord, I beg you to save me!"[86]

Christian went on like this for a great while, but the flames

---

[85] Ps. 69:14
[86] Eph. 6:18, Ps. 116:4

were still reaching for him. He also heard threatening voices and rushing about so that he thought he might be torn to pieces or trampled on like mud in the streets.

For the next several miles, these frightful sights and dreadful sounds continued until he heard what he thought was a gang of demons approaching. He stopped to carefully consider his next move. He already had half a mind to turn back, but on the other hand, he thought he might already be half-way through the valley by now. He also remembered how he had overcome so many other obstacles on the path, and the danger of going back might be much worse than going forward.

He made up his mind to move forward, yet the demons seemed to draw closer and closer. When it seemed as though they were almost on top of him, he cried out fervently, "I will walk in the strength of the Lord my God!"

With that, the demons turned back and did not bother him again.

It's important to note that poor Christian was so confused that he didn't know the sound of his own voice. Just when he came close to the mouth of the burning pit, one of the wicked ones sneaked up behind him whispering suggestions and deplorable blasphemies. Christian thought these voices had originated from his own mind, and it troubled him deeply. To think that he should now blaspheme the one he loved so much before weighed heavily on his heart. If he could have helped it, he never would have done it. Unfortunately, he did not have the discretion to stop listening to the voices or to understand the real source of these wicked thoughts.

While traveling in this depressed state for quite some time, he thought he heard a man's voice on the path ahead of him saying, "Though I walk through the Valley of the Shadow of

Death, I will fear no evil, for you are with me."[87]

Just hearing another's voice on this dreadful path filled him with joy for several reasons: first, because he now believed there were others who feared God in this valley like himself.

Secondly, he reasoned that God was with him as he traveled through this dark and dreary place even though he could not see Him.[88]

Thirdly, he hoped to catch up with the man so that he might enjoy fellowship with him as they traveled along the Way together. He called out to him, but the man did not answer because he thought he was alone too.

Finally, day broke and Christian said, "He has turned the shadow of death into the morning."[89]

In the light of a new day, he looked back, not out of any desire to return but rather to see the hazards he had navigated through in the dark. He could now see more clearly the ditch on one side and the quagmire on the other with the narrow path between them. He could also see the hobgoblins, satyrs, and dragons of the pit from a distance, but after daybreak, they were reluctant to come any closer. Yet he saw them according to that which is written, "He reveals deep things out of darkness and brings out to light the shadow of death."[90]

Christian's spirits were lifted to have made it this far through the dangerous valley, but even though these dangers were exposed by the light, he still feared them more than ever.

Fortunately, the rising sun offered another mercy to Christian. For without a doubt, the first part of the Valley of the Shadow of Death was dangerous, but the second part—which he was about to experience—was, if possible, far more

---

[87] Ps. 23:4
[88] Job 9:11
[89] Amos 5:8
[90] Job 12:22

dangerous.

This is because from where he stood now and all the way to the end of the valley was full of snares, traps, snags, nets, pitfalls, deep holes, and unsafe ledges. Had it been dark, like it was when he first entered the valley, even if he had a thousand souls, they would have all been lost. But as I said, the sun was now rising.

"His lamp shines on my head, and by His light I go through darkness,"[91] Christian said as he made it to the end of the valley by walking in the light.

I saw in my dream that at the end of the valley lay blood, bones, ashes, and mangled bodies of pilgrims that had gone this way earlier. While I was searching for a reason for this tragedy, I spotted a little cave ahead of me, where two giants, Pope and Pagan, lived in days past. It was by their power and tyranny that these men viciously murdered pilgrims that had traveled this way.

Christian went by this place without much danger, and I was curious as to why. Later I learned that Pagan had been dead for quite some time. As for the other, though he was alive, he had, because of his age and the many clever conflicts he encountered in his younger days, grown so senile and stiff in his joints that he could now do little more than sit in the mouth of the cave, grinning at pilgrims as they went by, frustrated that he could not confront them.

Christian went on his way, but he did not know what to think about the old man sitting at the mouth of the cave, especially since Pope did not come after him but said, "You will never be restored until more of you are burned!" To this, Christian was silent and just smiled as he passed by, unharmed and singing:

---

[91] Job 29:3

O world of wonders, (I can say no less,)
That I should be preserved in that distress
That I have met with here! O blessed be
That Hand that from it has delivered me!
Dangers in darkness, devils, Hell, and sin,
Did surround me, while I this vale was in;
Snares, and pits, and traps, and nets did lie
About my path, that worthless, silly I
Might have been caught, entangled, and cast down;
But since I live, let Jesus wear the crown.

Chapter Six

Temptation, Discontentment, and Shame

As Christian continued traveling on the Way, he came to a slight hill that allowed him to clearly see Faithful ahead of him.

Christian called out to him, "Hello! Look over here! Wait for me to catch up, and we can walk on this path together!"

Faithful heard him but kept walking, so Christian called out to him again, this time a little louder, "Hold up a minute so that I can catch up to you!"

Faithful kept walking but yelled back, "No, I cannot stop. My life is in danger for the avenger of blood is behind me."

Faithful's dedication to the path both encouraged and challenged Christian, so with all the strength he could muster, he began running as fast as he could, making every effort to catch up with Faithful quickly. In fact, he raced right past him so that the last became first! Christian smiled so proudly when he passed Faithful, that is, until he stumbled and fell to the ground because he was not paying attention to where he was going. He was unable to get back up until Faithful came to help him. The two felt great admiration and love for each other as they began a delightful conversation about all the things that had happened to them on their journeys.

Christian threw his arm around Faithful and patted him on

the back. "Faithful, I respect and love you as my own brother, and I'm so glad to have caught up with you. God has made our spirits one so that we can walk as companions on this pleasant Way."

Faithful turned and smiled. "Absolutely! In fact, you have been such a good friend to me that I had hoped we might leave from our hometown together. But you got started before me, so I traveled this far alone."

"How long did you stay in the City of Destruction before you set out after me on your pilgrimage?"

Faithful just shook his head. "Until I could stay no longer. Immediately after you left, there was a lot of talk that our town would soon be burned to the ground with fire from heaven!"

Christian shot a quick, almost surprised glance at Faithful. "Really? The town was *really* talking about this?"

"Yes! In fact, everyone was talking about it, at least for a while!"

"Incredible!" said Christian, feeling encouraged. "Then why did no one else come with you to escape the danger?"

Faithful shrugged his shoulders and said, "Like I said, there was a lot of talk going around, but I'm not sure many actually believed it. There were even heated debates in which I heard some people making fun of you and saying you were on a desperate journey. Oh, but I believed, and still do, that our town will be destroyed with fire and brimstone from above. So I decided in that moment to plan my escape!"

Christian's face grew concerned. "What have you heard about our good friend Pliable?"

"I heard that he followed you all the way until the Swamp of Despair. Many said that he fell in there, but he would never admit it, although it was obvious he did since he was covered with that kind of dirt."

"And how did his family and friends treat him?" Christian

asked.

Faithful just shook his head. "Since returning home, he's been the object of scorn and ridicule by everyone. They mock and despise him to the point that he's been unable to find work. He's now seven times worse than had he never left the city to begin with."

"I don't understand," Christian said with a puzzled look. "Why did they turn against him since he abandoned the Way and returned?"

"Oh, they've gone as far as to say, 'Hang him! He is a traitor and not true to his profession!' I think God has even stirred up His enemies to harass him and make him an example of someone who abandons the Way."[92]

Christian felt sorry for Pliable. "Were you able to talk to him before you left?"

"Unfortunately, no," Faithful said. "I ran across him once in the streets, but he crossed to the other side to try to avoid me because he was ashamed of what he had done."

"That's too bad," said Christian. "When we first set out, I had great hopes for Pliable, but now I fear that he will die when the city is destroyed. He's living out the proverb, 'A dog returns to its vomit, and a sow that is washed returns to her wallowing mud.'"[93]

Faithful agreed. "That's my fear for him too, but at this point, there's nothing more we can do."

"Well, Faithful," said Christian, "let's talk about something else—about things that concern us now. I want to know everything that has happened on your journey. I cannot imagine that you did not encounter some interesting things along the way."

---

[92] Jer. 29:18–19
[93] 2 Peter 2:22

Faithful thought for a moment then began. "Well, I escaped the swamp that I understand you fell into and made it all the way to the gate without much danger. However, I did encounter a woman named Wanton, also referred to as Promiscuous, who intended to harm me if she could."

Christian's eyes grew wide. "You were very fortunate to have escaped her net! She gave Joseph a lot of trouble. He also escaped her like you, but it almost cost him his life.[94] Tell me, what did she do to you?"

"You cannot imagine, unless you had been there, just how flattering she was." He then looked directly at Christian and said, "She did her best to persuade me to run away with her, promising me all sorts of pleasure and contentment."

Christian held up his hand. "But she did not promise you the satisfaction of a clear conscience."

"No. You know exactly what I mean," said Faithful slowly, "all manner of sexual satisfaction."

"Thank God you escaped her!" Christian said. "The man under the Lord's wrath falls into an adulterous woman's deep pit."[95]

"Well, I'm not sure whether I escaped her completely or not."

"Why? I'm assuming you did not give in to her desires."

"No, I did not defile myself," Faithful said, shaking his head. "I happened to remember an old writing that I had seen, which said, 'Her steps take hold on Hell.'[96] So I shut my eyes so that I would not be deceived by her beauty.[97] Eventually she realized that I was an unwilling participant in her game, so she

---

[94] Gen. 39:11–13
[95] Prov. 22:14
[96] Prov. 5:5
[97] Job 31:1

became angry with me and I went on my way."

Christian was eager to hear more about Faithful's journey. "Were you assaulted at any other time along the Way?"

"Yes," Faithful said. "When I arrived at the foot of the hill called Difficulty, I met a very old man who asked me my name and where I was going. I told him that I was a pilgrim heading to the Celestial City. He then said, 'You look like an honest man. Would you be interested in working for me for what I can pay you?'

"I asked him his name and where he lived. He said his name was Adam the First and that he lived in the town of Deceit.[98] I then asked him what line of business he was in and to provide more specifics about the wages he would pay. He told me that it was delightful work, and as for my pay, I would be the heir to his family!

"I continued asking him for more details about his home and others who worked for him. He told me that he lived in a luxurious home, more luxurious than any home in the world, and his only other workers were his children. I asked how many children he had, and he said that he had just three daughters, the Lust of the Flesh, the Lust of the Eyes, and the Pride of Life,[99] and that I could marry all of them if I wished. Then I asked how long I could live with him, and he told me as long as he lived himself."

Christian was captivated by the story and blurted out, "Well, what did you decide? Did you make an agreement with the old man?"

"Why, at first I found myself somewhat inclined to go with him! I thought about his offer, and it seemed fair. But as we talked, I noticed something written on his forehead that said,

---

98 Eph. 4:22
99 1 John 2:16

'Put off the old man with his deeds.'"

"What happened next?" Christian asked.

Faithful continued, "Well, it suddenly occurred to me that regardless of what he said or how much he offered, when he got me home, he would sell me as a slave! I insisted that he stop talking to me since I had no intentions of going near his home. Then he got very angry and told me that he would send someone else who would make my journey miserable to my soul.

"As I turned to leave, I felt him grab hold of my arm and pull me back with such deadly force that I thought he had pulled my arm completely off! I cried out, 'Oh, wretched man am I!'[100]

"I escaped and made my way up the hill. I was about half-way up when I looked back and saw a man coming after me as quick as the wind. He caught up with me just about the place where the shady arbor stands."

"I'm very familiar with that place," Christian said, interrupting. "It was there that I sat down to rest but was overcome with sleep and lost this certificate out of my chest pocket!"

Faithful held up his hand, stopping Christian. "Hold on a second, my friend, and hear me out." Then he continued, "As I said, the man caught up with me, and without saying much, he knocked me unconscious with one blow and left me for dead. When I somewhat revived, I asked him why he abused me so. He said it was because of my secret inclination to follow Adam the First. With that, he struck me another deadly blow in the chest and beat me down backward so that I lay at his feet dead, as before. When I recovered again, I pleaded with him for mercy, but he said, 'I do not know how to show mercy!' And with that, he knocked me back down again,

---

[100] Rom. 7:24

leaving me for dead. No doubt he would have killed me had another not come by and restrained him."

"Who was it that restrained him?" Christian asked.

"I did not know Him at first, but as He went by, I could see the holes in His hands and in His side. Then I concluded that He was our Lord. After this, I went up the hill."

Christian thought for a moment and then said, "That man who overtook you was Moses. He does not spare anyone nor does he know how to show mercy to those that violate the law."

"I know it very well," Faithful said, rubbing his chest where the man had struck him. "This was not my first encounter with him. Moses was the one who found me in the security of my own home in the City of Destruction and told me he would burn my house to the ground if I stayed there."

"But, Faithful," Christian said, "did you not see the Palace Beautiful on top of the hill right next to where you encountered Moses?"

"Oh sure!" Faithful nodded. "As I was coming up to it, I saw the lions too, but I think they were asleep. However, it was almost noon, and since I had so much of the day before me, I decided to pass by the porter and come down the hill."

"He told me that he saw you go by," Christian said. "I wish you had stopped at the house because you would have seen so many rare treasures that you never would have been able to forget."

They walked a little farther, and then Christian asked, "Please tell me, did you meet anyone else in the Valley of Humiliation?"

"Yes, I met a man named Discontent," Faithful said. "He was working hard trying to persuade me to go back with him because he said that I would lose all honor if I was to enter the Valley of Humiliation. He also told me that if I went into the valley, it would be against the wishes of all my friends, including Pride, Arrogance, Self-Conceit, Worldly Glory, and others, who, he was confident, would be highly offended if I made a fool of myself and ruined my reputation by entering the valley."

"Well, how did you answer him?"

"I told him that all of these men he named might claim to be my friends, and rightly so since they were actually my relatives," Faithful said, "but since I became a pilgrim, they have disowned me, and I have rejected them as if we had never been related.

"I also told him that he had quite misrepresented this valley because humility comes before honor and pride before destruction. Therefore, I told him I would rather go through this valley with the same honor of those who are wise than choose that which he esteemed more worthy."

"Did you meet with anyone else in the valley?"

"Yes, I did. I met a man named Shame, but of all the people I've met on my pilgrimage, I don't think his name suits him. I'm sure he would disagree, but a shameful person can change after feeling convicted of their sins and feels embarrassed by their actions. But Shame has no shame and will never change his ways. That's why I believe it is more correct to call him Shameless."

"Why, what did he say to you?" Christian asked.

"What did he say?" Faithful threw up his arms as if exasperated. "Why, he objected to religion itself! He said it was foolish business for a man to give any attention to religion. He even said that a tender conscience was an unmanly thing and that to be constantly watching everything you say or do just makes you weak and keeps more daring spirits from freely parading about like the heroes of this modern age.

"He then argued that only a few of the powerful, wealthy,

and intelligent people have ever believed what I do, and those that do are persuaded to become fools by voluntarily giving up their money for who knows what.[101] Then he objected to the low standard of living that many pilgrims submit themselves to and sneered at their ignorance and lack of understanding for new scientific theories.

"He continued berating me about many more things…like it was a shame to sit convicted and agonizing under a sermon or to be deeply concerned about eternal realities. Further, he said it was a shame to ask my neighbor for forgiveness for petty offenses or to make restitution if I have stolen from someone.

"He said it's not normal to become concerned over a few vices, which he called by different names because it made pilgrims a laughingstock to the educated and enlightened of the world. He then said that this type of thinking leads men to appreciate the poor and less fortunate simply because they belong to the same religious affiliation. Finally, he asked me, 'Is this not a shame?'"

"And what did you say to him?" asked Christian.

"Say? What could I say?" Faithful responded, exasperated. "To tell you the truth, I did not know what to say at first! He was pressing me so hard that I became ashamed and humiliated. And Shame brought up that which made me feel even more defeated. But at last, I began to consider that 'What is highly valued among men is detestable to God.'[102] Shame had told me what is acceptable by worldly men, but he told me nothing about what God desires or commands.

"I also thought about the Day of Judgment. We will not be designated to life or death according to the standards of this world but according to the wisdom and law of the most High

---

[101] 1 Cor. 1:26, 3:18; Phil. 3:7–9; John 7:48
[102] Luke 16:15

God. "Therefore, I thought, what God says is best is indeed best, though all the men in the world are against it.

"Seeing, then, that God prefers His religion and that He prefers a tender conscience, that those that make themselves fools for the kingdom of Heaven are wise, and that the poor man that loves Christ is richer than the greatest man in the world that hates Him, I told Shame to leave me since he was an enemy of my salvation! Why should I continue to listen to him disparage my Sovereign Lord? How, then, could I look Him in the face at His coming?[103] How can I expect to receive His blessing if I'm now ashamed of His ways and my fellow believers?

"Nevertheless, Shame proved to be a bold villain whom I could scarcely shake off. He kept following me around like a shadow, constantly whispering in my ear about one thing or another regarding the weaknesses that accompany true religion. Finally, I told him that it was pointless for him to continue in this manner because the things that he despised I found glorious. When I had finally shaken him off, I began to sing,

The trials that those men do meet with,
Who are obedient to the heavenly call,
Are manifold, and suited to the flesh,
And come, and come, and come again afresh;
That now, or some time else, we by them may
Be taken, overcome, and cast away.
O let the pilgrims, let the pilgrims then,
Be vigilant and quit themselves like men."

---

[103] Mark 8:38

Christian compassionately embraced Faithful. "My brother, I'm glad that you bravely withstood the attacks of this villain. As you said, of all the people you met, he undoubtedly has the wrong name. How bold is he to follow us in the streets and attempt to shame us before the world, that is, to make us ashamed of that which is good. If he were not so audacious, he would never attempt to do as he does. But let us continue to resist him, for aside from his boasting, he is nothing more than a fool. 'The wise shall inherit glory,' said Solomon, 'but He holds up fools to shame.'"[104]

"I think we must cry to Him for help against Shame that we would be brave for truth on the earth," said Faithful.

"Yes, this is true. Did you meet anybody else in that valley?"

"No, I did not. In fact, I had sunshine all the rest of the way through it as well as through the Valley of the Shadow of Death."

"Then the valley was far better for you than what I experienced for it was much worse for me," Christian said. "Almost as soon as I entered the Valley of Humiliation, I found myself in a dreadful battle with that foul demon Apollyon. I truly thought he was going to kill me, especially when he got me down and crushed me under him almost to pieces. Then he threw me, and my sword flew out of my hand. He told me that he was going to kill me, but I cried out to God, and He heard me and delivered me out of all my troubles. Then I entered the Valley of the Shadow of Death and had no light for almost half the way through it. I thought I would have been killed there many times, but at last day broke, the sun rose, and I went through the rest of the valley with far more ease and peace."

---

[104] Prov. 3:35

The Hypocrisy of Talkative

As the two continued on their journey, they came to a wide place in the road. Faithful glanced to one side and saw a man walking alongside them, although some distance away. His name was Talkative, and he was a tall man and somewhat better looking from a distance than up close.

Faithful introduced himself by calling out to him, "Say there, friend, where you going? Is it to the heavenly country?"

"Yes, that's where I'm heading," Talkative replied.

"Wonderful!" Faithful exclaimed. "We would be happy if you were to join us on the journey."

Talkative quickly blurted out, "Gladly! I would love to join you!"

"Then come on over," Faithful said with a gesturing wave. "Let's spend our time talking about things worthwhile."

Talkative came running over and started walking next to Faithful. "Having a worthwhile discussion with you or anyone else sounds good to me," Talkative said. "I'm so glad to have met up with pilgrims who want to have these types of conversations. To tell you the truth, I've not found many who do. In fact, most would rather talk about things that benefit no one, and this has often concerned me."

Faithful nodded in agreement. "I completely understand your concern for there's nothing better in all the world than talking about our Heavenly Father."

"I like what you are saying for you speak with strong conviction," Talkative said with a wink, signifying his approval. "And I agree, there's nothing more enjoyable and worthwhile than talking about the things of God. What gives a man more satisfaction than to enjoy wonderful things? For instance, if a man enjoys talking about history or mysterious things or of miracles, wonders, or signs, he will not find them more delightfully and as carefully recorded as in the Holy Scriptures."

"That's true," said Faithful, holding up a finger, "but our real purpose is to *benefit* from talking about such things. That should be our focus."

"That's exactly what I was about to say," Talkative said, as if he had already thought of it himself. "Because it's in these worthwhile conversations that we learn about a lot of topics, including worldly pride and heavenly joys. For instance, generally speaking, we might learn about the necessity of the new birth, the insufficiency of our works, the need for Christ's righteousness, and so forth. And we will also learn what it means to repent, believe, pray, suffer, and more, all while finding great comfort in the promises of the gospel. And that's not all! We might also learn to refute false opinions, to confirm the truth, and to instruct the ignorant."

"All this is true, and I'm glad to hear you say such things," said Faithful.

Then Talkative shook his head in disapproval. "Unfortunately, this lack of knowledge is why so few people understand the need for faith and the necessity of the work of grace in their heart in order to obtain eternal life. As a result, they live ignorantly by the works of the law, which by no means can a man be saved."

"Excuse me," Faithful said, trying to get a word in.

"Heavenly knowledge of these truths is a gift of God. No man can attain this knowledge by human effort, let alone by *just* talking about them."

"I know all of this very well!" Talkative said, slapping Faithful on the back. "For a man can receive nothing except what has been given to him from Heaven. All is of grace, not of works. I could quote you a hundred Scripture passages confirming this."

"Well, then," said Faithful, "what do you consider a worthwhile topic for us to discuss right now?"

"Whatever you would like!" Talkative said, shrugging his shoulders. "I will talk about things that are heavenly or earthly, moral or evangelical, sacred or profane, past or future, foreign or domestic, essential or incidental provided any such discussion is worthwhile."

Talkative quickly impressed Faithful with his fluent words and contagious enthusiasm, so Faithful stepped aside to speak with Christian privately as he had been walking alone all this time. He lowered his voice and said, "What a brave companion we have here! Surely this man will make a very excellent pilgrim."

Christian smiled modestly and said, "This man that you are so captivated with can charm anyone he meets."

Faithful was surprised. "Then you know him?"

"Know him?" said Christian with his wide eyes. "Oh yes, better than he knows himself."

Faithful glanced back at Talkative walking behind them and said, "Then, seriously, tell me who he is."

"His name is Talkative, and he lives in our hometown. I'm surprised that you do not know him, but of course it is a rather large town."

"Who is his father, and where does he live?"

"He is the son of Say-well and lives on Foolish-Talk Row. Everyone who knows him calls him Talkative of Foolish-Talk Row. And despite his eloquent speech, he's a repulsive person."

"Well, he seems to be a rather charming man," said Faithful, glancing back at Talkative again.

"That he is to those that are not acquainted with him. He appears good at a distance, but up close, he is quite the opposite. Your description of him reminds me of a painting that's best seen from a distance as up close it becomes noticeably unpleasing."

Faithful started to laugh. "I'm beginning to think you're not serious since you were smiling."

"Even though I smiled, God forbid that I should joke or make a false accusation about this man!" said Christian in a very serious tone. "Let me tell you a little more about him. Talkative does not care what company he keeps or what they discuss. Just as he's talking with you now, he freely talks in the tavern, and the more he drinks, the more he talks. Faith and religion have no place in his heart, home, or conversation. He's a liar, and his religion rests merely in what he says."

"If this is so, then I've been greatly deceived by this man," said Faithful.

"Deceived? You may be sure of it!" Christian said emphatically. "Remember the proverb, 'Do not do what they do, for they do not practice what they preach. For the kingdom of God is not a matter of talk but of power.'[105] He talks of prayer, repentance, faith, and the new birth, but he only knows how to talk about them.

"I have been with his family and have observed him both at home and abroad, and I know what I say about him is the truth.

---

[105] Matt. 23:3, 1 Cor. 4:20

His home is as empty of true religion as an egg white is of flavor. There's neither prayer nor any sign of repentance for sin there. The truth is, an animal serves God far better than he does. To all who know him, he is the very stain, reproach, and shame of religion.[106] No one has a good word to say about him in the neighborhood where he lives. The lowest of society, who know him best, say that he's a saint abroad and a devil at home.

"Even his poor family would agree with me. He's impolite, mean-spirited, and unreasonable with his servants. They are at a loss for how to speak with him, much less how to work for him. Those who have any business with him say that it's better to deal with barbarian traders than with him because they will be treated more fairly. For Talkative would, if possible, go behind their backs to defraud, deceive, and cheat them.

"As you can imagine, he raises his sons to follow in his footsteps. If he notices that any of them appear foolish, weak, or insecure, he calls them fools and blockheads. For this reason, he will not employ them or even provide a recommendation for them to others. In my opinion, his wicked lifestyle has caused many to stumble and fall, and he will be the ruin of many more, unless God prevents it."

Faithful was dumbfounded. "Well, my brother, I am bound to believe you, not only because you say you know him but also because you can offer your report with a good Christian attitude. I cannot imagine you would say these things out of ill will but rather because it's the truth."

"Had I met him now, just like you, I might have thought of him the way you did at first," said Christian. "Or, if I had received this information from the hands of enemies of true religion, I would have thought it was slander from wicked men that desire to damage the name and reputation of good men.

---

[106] Rom. 2:24–25

But I can prove that he is guilty of all these things and much more that are equally as bad. Besides, good men are ashamed of him. They can neither call him brother nor friend and are embarrassed to even say they know him."

"Well," said Faithful, feeling a little foolish, "I see that words and actions are two different things, and from now on, I will better observe this difference."

"They really are two separate things. In fact, they are as different as the body is from the spirit," said Christian. "Perhaps it would help if you thought about it like this: The body without the spirit is dead, so the same can be said about words without action. The spirit of true faith is a transformed life. It's written that 'Religion that God our Father accepts as pure and faultless is this: to look after orphans and widows in their distress and to keep oneself from being polluted by the world.'"[107]

Christian glanced back at Talkative, who was still walking behind them. "Talkative is not aware of this truth. He thinks that hearing and speaking makes a good Christian and therefore deceives his own spirit. Hearing is like the sowing of the seed, and talking alone is not enough to prove that fruit is indeed part of the heart and life. We can be sure that on the Day of Judgment, men will be judged according to their fruit.[108] No one will say then, 'Did you believe?' but rather, 'Were you doers or talkers only?' and they will be judged accordingly. The end of the world is compared to our earthly harvest,[109] and you know that men at harvest want nothing but fruit and grain. But know that nothing will be accepted that's not faith. I say all of this to show you how insignificant Talkative's profession will be at that day."

---

[107] James 1:27
[108] Matt. 13:23
[109] Matt. 13:30

Faithful thought carefully and then said, "This reminds me of what Moses wrote when he described the animal that's ceremonially clean as having a split hoof and chews the cud.[110] However, the animal that only has a split hoof or chews only the cud is not clean. For example, the rabbit chews the cud but is unclean because it does not have a split hoof. Talkative is like the rabbit that chews the cud; that is, he seeks knowledge and chews on the Word, but he does not have a split hoof— rather, he does not separate himself from a sinful lifestyle. Like the rabbit, he retains the foot of the dog or bear, and so he's unclean."

Christian smiled and said, "I believe you're speaking the true sense of the gospel. Let me add something else from the Apostle Paul. He calls some men, including those great talkers, resounding gongs and clanging cymbals.[111] In another place, he describes them as noisy and lifeless.[112] They are a soul without a life and without the true faith and grace of the gospel. As a result, they will never be found in the Kingdom of Heaven among those that are the children of life, even if they have the voice of an angel."

"Well, I was not so fond of his company before, but now I'm sick of it!" Faithful said in disgust. "What should we do to get rid of him?"

Christian had an idea and leaned in close to Faithful. "Take my advice and do as I tell you. If this works, you'll find that he will soon be sick of your company too, unless God should touch his heart and change him."

"What do you suggest?" asked Faithful.

"Go over to him and start a serious discussion about the power of true faith. Once he has agreed to this, and he will, ask

---

[110] Lev. 11, Deut. 14
[111] 1 Cor. 13:1–3
[112] 1 Cor. 14:7

115

him clearly whether this power has been found in his heart, home, or lifestyle."

So Faithful walked over to Talkative and said, "Say there, how are you now?"

"I'm doing great, thank you," Talkative said somewhat tersely. "However, I thought we would be much farther along in conversation by now."

"Well, if you want, we can talk now," Faithful responded more directly. "Since you suggested that I pick the topic, how about this—how does the grace of God reveal itself in one who has been saved?"

Talkative smiled and said, "So it seems as though you want to talk about the power of things. Well, this is a very good question, and I'm more than willing to provide you a brief answer. First, when one has been saved by the grace of God, it causes in him a great outcry against sin. Secondly..."

"Hold on a moment!" Faithful interjected, holding up his hand. "Let's consider each answer one at a time. I think that what you should say instead is that grace displays itself in a person by persuading the heart to hate sin."

Talkative quickly shot back, "Why? I don't see the difference between crying out against sin and hating sin."

"Oh, but there's a big difference!" Faithful said. "Someone can cry out against sin in principle but cannot hate sin unless they have a profound godly aversion to it. I've heard many cry out against sin from the pulpit who do not live it out in their heart, home, and lifestyle. Take, for example, Potiphar's wife. She cried out loudly as if she were godly and virtuous but would have committed adultery with Joseph in a heartbeat![113] Some cry out against sin while condoning it in their own lives. It's like a mother who scolds the child in her lap when it's

---

[113] Gen. 39:15

behaving badly but then immediately begins to hug and embrace the same child."

Talkative seemed caught off guard and was wondering what Faithful's angle might be. "It seems as though you're trying to be clever and set a trap for me."

"No, not at all!" Faithful said with his hand over his heart. "I'm only setting things right. But tell me, what was the second evidence that you were going to offer that displays how the grace of God reveals itself in one who has been saved?"

Talkative paused and then hesitantly answered, "A great knowledge of gospel mysteries."

"You should have mentioned this evidence first, but regardless, it's still not accurate," Faithful said, correcting him. "Great knowledge may be found in the mysteries of the gospel without any work of grace in the soul. You see, if a man has all knowledge, he may still not be a child of God.[114] When Christ said, 'Do you understand all these things?' and the disciples answered, 'Yes,' He added, 'Blessed are you who *do* them.' Christ does not lay the blessing in the mere *understanding* of them but in the *doing* of them. For a person can understand something and still not act on it. It's like the servant that understands what his master wants and still fails to act on it. A man may have the knowledge of an angel and yet not be a Christian at all. Therefore, your evidence is not true.

"Indeed, to possess knowledge pleases talkers and braggers, but to act on that knowledge pleases God. That's not to say that the heart can be without knowledge, for without knowledge, the heart is nothing. In fact, there are two types of knowledge. The first type of knowledge is based in the mere study of the world and serves just the student. The second type of knowledge combines grace with faith and love and leads a

---

[114] 1 Cor. 13:2

man to act on the will of God from his heart, providing him contentment. As it is written, 'Give me understanding, so that I may keep your law and obey it with all my heart.'[115]

Talkative was quickly becoming irritated. "You've set a trap for me again! This has not been the pleasing conversation that I thought it would be."

Faithful calmly replied, "Well then, do offer more clear evidence that displays the work of grace in the heart."

Talkative folded his arms. "No, not at this time, because I can see that we will not agree."

"Well, if you won't," said Faithful, "then will you allow me to do so?"

"Fine! You are free to do so," Talkative said, waving his hands in the air.

Then Faithful began, "A true work of grace in the heart is easily recognized by the person that has it or by others that are observing him. For the person that has it, he finds himself under conviction for his sin, especially concerning the defilement of his own body. He's also convicted for the sin of unbelief, for which he is sure to be damned unless he finds mercy at God's hand through faith in Jesus Christ. The knowledge of sin and his inward convictions cause him to feel sorrow and shame.[116]

"But then he finds Jesus Christ as his Savior and the absolute necessity of living for and with Him for the rest of his life. And when he does, he experiences a hunger and thirst for Him based on the promise, 'blessed are those who hunger and thirst for righteousness and they will be filled.'

"Now, based on the strength or weakness of his faith in his Savior, he experiences joy and peace, a love for holiness, and

---

[115] Ps. 119:34
[116] Ps. 38:18, Jer. 31:19, John 16:8, Rom. 7:24, Mark 16:16, Gal. 2:16

118

a desire to know Him more and serve Him in this world. But even as all of this is revealed to him, his old self and inability to reason misjudge the matter, and he is unable to fully understand this work of grace. Therefore, before he can conclude with confidence that this is a work of grace, the one experiencing this work must make a very sound judgment."[117]

Faithful could tell that Talkative was becoming irritated as he continued with his second point. "To others observing this man, this work of grace is evident by a genuine confession of faith in Christ and by living a life that agrees with his confession. This includes living a life of holiness in himself, in his family, and in his lifestyle. This holiness teaches him to inwardly condemn his sin and doing it in secret. It also teaches him to suppress sin in his family and to promote holiness in the world. He does so not by just talking about it, as a hypocrite or talkative person might do, but by practical application in faith and love to the power of the Word.[118]

"And now," concluded Faithful, "do you have any objections to this brief description of the work of grace and to the evidence provided? If not, then let me pose another question."

"No, I have no objections and nothing more to say. I'm just listening, so ask your second question," Talkative said with little enthusiasm.

Faithful compassionately leaned in close to Talkative. "My question is this: Have you experienced the first part of the description of a true work of grace in your heart, and does your life and conversation testify to that same experience? Or is your religion based just on the things you talk about without little care for your behavior?

---

[117] John 16:9, Gal. 2:15–16, Acts 4:12, Matt. 5:6, Rev. 21:6
[118] Job 42:5–6; Ps. 50:23; Ezek. 20:43; Matt. 5:8; John 14:15; Rom. 10:10; Ezek. 36:25; Phil 1:27, 3:17–20

"Please, if you answer me, only say what you know God will agree with and that your conscience can justify. It's not the person that commends himself that is approved but rather he whom the Lord commends. Besides, to say that you're one way, when your conversation and all your neighbors say otherwise, is a lie and wicked."

At first, Talkative was embarrassed, but he quickly regained his composure. "You come now in your own experience and conscience before God and appeal to Him for justification of what you said. I did not expect this kind of conversation nor am I ready to answer your questions, because I'm not accountable to you, that is, unless you have also taken it upon yourself to be my religious examiner. And even if you did, I would refuse to make you my judge. What I really want to know is, why have you decided to ask me such questions?"

Faithful said very directly, "Because I invited you to talk but then realized that you had no basis for your words. And to be completely honest, your reputation precedes you as a man who talks a great deal about religion but whose lifestyle is hypocritical. They say you are a blemish among Christians and that true religion suffers on account of your ungodly conduct. I have heard that some have already stumbled because of your wicked ways and that more are in danger of having their faith destroyed because of the way you practice your religion. Your religion involves meeting at a tavern and promotes covetousness, uncleanness, swearing, lying, bad company, and more. The proverb that describes a prostitute is also true of you; in that she is a shame to all women, so are you a shame to all believers."

Talkative stopped walking and said, "Since you are so quick to listen to stories about me and to judge so rashly, I can only conclude that you are an irritable, sad man who is not worthy of talking to anyway. So goodbye!" He then turned and walked away.

Noticing that Talkative had left, Christian came up to his brother and said, "Did I not tell you what would happen? Your words and his desires could not agree. Talkative would rather leave your company than change his life. But he's gone, and I say, let him go. The loss is his own, and he has saved us the trouble of leaving him because, I assume, he would eventually ruin our reputation. Besides, the apostle says, 'Separate yourself from such people.'"[119]

"Yes, but I'm glad I was able to talk even briefly with him," said Faithful. "Who knows, maybe he will think more about what I clearly presented to him, but if he does not, I'm innocent of his blood."

Christian nodded in agreement. "You spoke very plainly to him. Unfortunately, very few believers are that faithful in dealing with people these days, giving true religion a bad smell. Instead, we find talkative fools that can only speak about faith and whose hearts are morally corrupt and proud. Their claim to faith confuses the world, places a stain on Christianity, and grieves those that are sincere in their faith. I wish that all believers would deal with such people as you've done. Then perhaps they might come to a better understanding of true religion or find the company of believers too unbearable for them to remain."

Then Faithful said, "How Talkative showed off everything he knew at first! How bravely he spoke! How he presumed to drive down all before him! But no sooner than I started talking about the workings of grace in the heart, he walked off into the sunset. It will be the same for everyone except those that understand how the heart works."

---

[119] 2 Cor. 6:17

Evangelist Warns of the Coming Tribulation

They continued traveling on the Way, talking about everything they had seen, which helped pass the time since they were now walking through a wilderness. When they were almost out of this wilderness, Faithful happened to glance back and saw a man that he recognized coming up behind them and said, "Hey, Christian, look who's catching up with us!"

Christian looked back and was immediately filled with joy. "It's my good friend Evangelist!"

"Yes, and my good friend too!" said Faithful with a big smile. "He was the one who put me on the path to the Wicket Gate!"

When Evangelist walked up, he greeted them, saying, "Peace be with you, my dear friends! And peace to those who have helped you along the way."

"Welcome, welcome, my good friend!" Christian said, embracing him. "Just seeing you again reminds me of your earlier kindness and tireless work for my eternal good."

"And let me add a thousand times welcome!" Faithful said, shaking Evangelist's hand vehemently. "How sweet and desirable your company is to us poor pilgrims!"

"How have you been doing, my friends, since we last parted ways?" asked Evangelist. "What have you encountered, and how have you conducted yourselves?"

Christian and Faithful told him of all the things that had happened to them on their journey, including the many difficulties they had encountered to get to this point.

"I am so glad to hear it!" said Evangelist. "Not glad that you were met with trials but that despite your many weaknesses, you were victorious over those trials and made it this far on the Way.

"Again, I'm so happy, both for my own sake as well as yours. I have sown, and you have reaped. The day is coming when both those that sow and reap will rejoice together.[120] That is, of course, if you do not become weary of the Christian life but hold out to the end.[121] The crown is in front of you, and it's one that will last forever. Run in a way that you will obtain it.[122] Some people have set out for the crown, but after they have traveled a great distance to reach it, another steps in and takes it from them. Hold on to what you have, and do not let any man take your crown.[123] You are not yet out of the gunshot range of the devil, and in your struggle against sin, you have not resisted to the point of shedding your blood. Always keep the kingdom in front of you, and believe without wavering the things that are invisible. Let nothing in this world get between you and your crown.

"Above all, pay attention to your own hearts and to the lusts inside you for they are deceitful above all things and desperately wicked. Set your face with a flint-like resolve since you have all power in heaven and earth on your side."

Christian thanked him for his counsel and encouragement and asked him to consider continuing this discussion as they all traveled together on the Way. Both Christian and Faithful

---

[120] John 4:36
[121] Gal. 4:9
[122] 1 Cor. 9:24–27
[123] Rev. 3:11

knew that he was a prophet and believed he could tell them of things that might happen to them and how they might resist and overcome them.

Evangelist agreed, and as they continued their journey, he began to tell them of things to come. "My sons, you have heard in the words in the truth of the gospel that you must go through many tribulations to enter the kingdom of heaven. You've also heard that in every city, imprisonment and afflictions await you. You cannot travel much farther without encountering them in one way or another. In fact, you've already experienced a measure of this truth, and more will immediately follow.

"As you can see, you're almost out of this wilderness, and soon you will come to a town that will appear directly before you. In that town, you will be severely assaulted by enemies who will make every attempt to kill you. You can be sure that one or both of you must seal the testimony that you hold with blood. But if you're faithful, even to the point of death, the King will give you a crown of life.

"Whoever dies there, although his death will be unnatural and quite painful, he will have the advantage over his companion, not only because he will arrive at the Celestial City first but because he will escape many miseries that the other will meet with in the rest of his journey.

"When you arrive in this town and find everything that I have said fulfilled, remember your friend, be courageous, and commit yourselves to God, your faithful Creator, while continuing to do what is right."

Chapter Seven
On Trial at Vanity Fair

Then I saw in my dream that when Christian and Faithful came out of the wilderness, they soon saw a town ahead of them named Vanity. At this town, there was a fair called Vanity Fair that was promoted all year long. It bore the name Vanity Fair for its preoccupation with idle pleasures and an over-the-top lifestyle and also because everything that was sold there, as well as those that came to buy, was vain, empty, and meaningless.[124] As is the saying of the wise man, "Everything in this world is meaningless!"[125]

This fair was not a new business but rather had been around for a very long time. Let me tell you how it began.

Almost five thousand years ago, there were pilgrims walking to the Celestial City, just like Christian and Faithful. Beelzebub, Apollyon, and Legion, along with their companions, knew the pilgrim's path would take them through the town of Vanity, so they set out to construct a year-round fair there. According to their plan, they would sell and promote all sorts of vanity amid a host of festivities, lasting all year long.

At this fair, you could purchase houses, land, trades, places,

---

[124] Ps. 62:9
[125] Eccl. 1:2–14, 2:11–17, 11:8; Isa. 40:17

honors, promotions, titles, countries, kingdoms, lusts, and pleasures. There were also delights of all sorts, such as prostitutes, wives, husbands, children, masters, servants, lives, blood, bodies, souls, silver, gold, pearls, precious stones, and much more.

If this was not enough, there was constant, round-the-clock entertainment, like jugglers, cheats, games, plays, clowns, mimics, swindlers, scoundrels, and a variety of amusements of every kind. Here, visitors would also find—without cost— offerings that included thefts, murders, adulteries, and perjuries, and all of them were available in various shades of blood red.

As with other fairs of less significance, there were many avenues and streets with names based on what type of merchandise was sold there. In the same way, there were places, avenues, and streets named after countries and kingdoms where the merchandise of the fair could quickly be found. There was British Avenue, French Avenue, Italian Avenue, Spanish Avenue, and German Avenue, all of which offered a variety of vanities for sale. But as with other fairs, where one commodity seems to dominate the entire market, such was the merchandise of Rome, which was the most sought after at the fair due to its lavish promotion. However, some, like our English nation, had expressed a disliking of Rome's crass peddling and promotion.

Now, as I said, the way to the Celestial City ran directly through Vanity, where this lively fair was located. Those that desire to go to the Celestial City and yet avoid going to this town would have to leave the world.

The King of Kings Himself, when traveling in this region, passed through Vanity on His way to His own country. It was a time when the fair was in full operation. I believe it was Beelzebub, the chief ruler of the fair, who invited Him to buy some of his vanities, and he would have made Him the lord of the fair if He would have only worshipped him as He went through the town.

Because the King was such an honorable person, Beelzebub led Him from street to street and showed him all the kingdoms of the world in a short time so that he might, if possible, lure the Blessed One to lower Himself and buy some of his vanities. But the King had no desire for any of the merchandise and therefore left the town without spending so much as one penny on any of these worthless things.[126] As you can see, this was a very old and well-established fair and a very renowned fair at that.

Now as I said, it was necessary for Christian and Faithful to pass through the fair in order to reach the Celestial City. But as they entered the fair, a loud and raucous crowd drew around them and became disturbed by the two men. This happened for several reasons.

First, both Christian and Faithful were dressed quite differently from the attire of those at the fair. The people just stared at them, calling them fools, lunatics, and strange men.[127]

Secondly, just as the crowd wondered at their clothing, they were also curious about their speech since few could understand what they said. Naturally, Christian and Faithful spoke the language of those following the Lord God Almighty, but the men running the fair only spoke the language of the world. From one end of the fair to the other, Christian and Faithful seemed almost barbaric to those in the town.[128]

Thirdly, and this especially disturbed the merchants, these pilgrims placed such little value on all the merchandise being sold. They did not care so much as to even look at them, and if someone called upon them to buy, they would put their

---

[126] Matt 4:8–9, Luke 4:5–7

[127] 1 Cor. 4:9–10

[128] 1 Cor 2:7–8

fingers in their ears, look upward, and cry, "Turn my eyes away from looking at these worthless things!" signifying that their trade and commerce were in heaven.[129]

One merchant observed their strange behavior and mocked them, saying, "What do you want to buy?"

But they looked at him seriously and said, "We buy the truth."[130]

This response just made the men of the fair despise Christian and Faithful even more. Some mocked, some taunted, and some slandered them, while others suggested they should be beaten. This all led to a great uproar, creating a state of confusion at the fair. Word spread quickly to the governor of the fair, who came down and appointed some of his most trusted advisors to interrogate the men responsible for almost destroying the fair.

So Christian and Faithful were brought under investigation. Those who presided over the proceedings asked where they came from, where they were going, and why they were so unusually dressed.

Christian and Faithful told them they were pilgrims and strangers in the world and that they were traveling to their own country, which was the heavenly Jerusalem.[131] They stated that they had given no reason for the men of the town or the merchants to abuse or delay them on their journey except that when asked what they wanted to buy, they said they would buy the truth.

But those who were appointed to interrogate them did not believe them to be any more than lunatics and madmen who came for the sole purpose of throwing the fair into confusion. Therefore, they beat them, smeared them with dirt, and put

---

[129] Ps. 119:37, Phil. 3:20–21
[130] Prov. 23:23
[131] Heb. 11:13–16

them into a cage as a spectacle for all the fair to see. They laid in the cage for some time and were made the objects of anyone's sport, malice, and revenge, all while the governor of the fair constantly laughed at all that happened to them.

Christian and Faithful were patient and did not return insult for insult but rather blessed those physically hurting them. They even spoke good words for bad and showed kindness despite their injuries.

There were some men at the fair who observed Christian and Faithful's actions. They were more sympathetic than most and became upset with those men who continually abused the prisoners.

But this just made the abusers even more violent. They flew into a furious rage at their accusers, claiming they were as bad as the caged prisoners and worthy of the same treatment.

Those who defended the pilgrims replied that as far as they could see, these men were quiet, sensible, and harmless. As far as they were concerned, there were many others that traded at the fair that were far more worthy to be caged and imprisoned than the two men they had abused. Both sides continued to debate the facts until they began to physically assault and injure one another. This happened all while Christian and Faithful acted very wisely and sensibly the entire time.

This uproar led to the two prisoners being brought once again before their interrogators and charged with creating a disturbance at the fair. As punishment, they were beat unmercifully, placed in iron shackles, and paraded around in chains up and down the streets of the fair as an example and warning to others that might dare speak on their behalf or associate with them.

Despite the public shame and disgrace they endured, Christian and Faithful continued to act wisely. Their humility and patience won over several of the men in the fair to their side. The number was few in comparison to the rest, but it only enraged their enemies to the point of demanding the death penalty as they claimed, "This cage and its irons are not a sufficient punishment for the damage they've done as well as deceiving the men of the fair. Therefore, they deserve death!"

Christian and Faithful were once again ordered back to the cage and their feet placed in stocks pending a trial.

During this time, both men recalled the prophecy of their faithful friend Evangelist, who claimed that both would suffer and at least one would die. They comforted each other, knowing that whoever was put to death would have the advantage. In their hearts, each man secretly desired the opportunity, but they committed themselves to the wise and sovereign purposes of God and remained content in their present condition while awaiting their fate.

When a convenient time was determined, they were brought forth for their trial in order to be found guilty and condemned. When the time had come, they were brought before their enemies in court and arraigned. The judge who presided over the trial was Lord Hate-good. The indictment was essentially the same as before but had been modified slightly to read, "That Faithful and Christian were enemies to and disturbers of the Fair. That they had made commotions and caused divisions in the town and had won a party over to their own most dangerous opinions, in contempt of the law of their prince."

Then Faithful responded to the indictment that he had only spoke out against that which had asserted itself higher than the Highest. "And as for causing any disturbance," he went on to say, "I made none, being myself a man of peace. As for the men who were won over to our sentiments, well, they were won because they saw the truth and believed us to be innocent. Now they have turned from their worse condition to the better. As to the prince you talk about, since he is Beelzebub, the enemy of our Lord, I defy him and all his angels."

Then it was proclaimed that anyone who had anything to say in support of their lord the king against the prisoner at the bar should appear immediately and provide evidence. Three witnesses came forward: Envy, Superstition, and Flatterer. They were asked if they knew the prisoner at the bar and what they had to say before their lord the king against him.

Envy eagerly stepped forward, took the stand, and said something to this effect: "Your honor, I have known this man a long time and will testify under oath before this honorable bench that he is…"

"Stop!" the judge said, quickly raising his hand. "First, swear him in." They swore him in, and Envy continued.

"Your honor, this man, despite his credible name, is one of the vilest men in our country. He shows no regard for our prince, our people, our laws, or our customs. Instead, he does all he can to persuade all men with his disloyal notions, which he refers to as principles of faith and holiness. And, in particular, I myself heard him once claim that Christianity and the customs of our town of Vanity contradicted each other and could not be reconciled. By his very words, your honor, he not only condemns our praiseworthy good deeds but also us in doing them."

Then the judge asked him, "Do you have anything more to say?"

"Your honor, I could say much more, only I would not want to tire the court," Envy responded with a slight smile. "However, if necessary, after the other gentlemen have testified, to avoid any lack of evidence that might allow the prisoner to go free, I would be willing to provide even more testimony at that time." He was told to stand by in case further testimony was needed.

Next they called Superstition to the stand and swore him in, asking, "What can you say for your lord the king against this prisoner?"

Superstition, who is also known as False Devotion, glared in the direction of Faithful and began, "Your honor, I'm not friends with this man nor do I desire to know him any better. However, I do know that he's a very dangerous man just from a conversation that I had with him in town the other day. During this conversation, I heard him say that our religion was in vain and that in no way could it ever please God."

Turning his attention to the judge, Superstition continued, "Now, your honor, you know very well the natural result of following such a claim; if our worship is in vain, then our sins are not forgiven, and therefore we are damned. This is my testimony against him."

Then Flatterer was sworn in and asked what he knew in support of their lord the king against the prisoner at the bar.

"Your honor and all of you gentlemen," began Flatterer, who was eager to please the court and those in attendance. "I've known this man for a long time and have heard him say things that should never be spoken. He has denounced our noble prince Beelzebub and has spoken shamefully of his honorable friends, including the Lord Old Man, the Lord Carnal Delight, the Lord Luxurious, the Lord Desire of Vain Glory, my old Lord Lusty, and Sir Having Greedy, along with all the rest of our noble leaders."

Flatterer paused as if for effect then continued, "Moreover, he has said that if all men thought just as he did then not one of these noblemen would remain any longer in this town. And besides that, he has not been afraid to severely criticize you, your honor, who is now appointed to be his judge. He has called you an ungodly villain, along with many other slanderous names with which he has smeared the good names of most of the nobility of our town."

When Flattery had finished testifying against Faithful, the

judge turned his attention to the prisoner at the bar and angrily spat, "You rebel, heretic, and traitor! Have you heard what these honest gentlemen have testified against you?"

Faithful very calmly replied, "May I speak a few words in my own defense?"

"You scoundrel!" the judge said, almost coming out of his seat. "You don't deserve to live any longer but to be put to death immediately right here on the spot!" Then the judge calmed down and said almost reluctantly, "However, so that all men may see our gentleness toward you, let's hear what you, a wicked renegade, have to say."

"First, I will reply to what Mr. Envy has testified," Faithful said as he began his defense. "I never said anything except to say that whatever rules, laws, customs, or people that are plainly against the Word of God would also directly contradict Christianity. If I have said anything that is incorrect, please point out my error and convince me otherwise. For I'm more than willing to recant it if you can prove it."

Faithful glanced over at Superstition. "Secondly, I will address the charge that Mr. Superstition brought against me. I can only say this: that for true worship of God, a divine faith is required, but there can be no divine faith without a divine revelation of the will of God. Therefore, anything added to the worship of God that's not in agreement with divine revelation is nothing but human faith, which will not result in eternal life."

Faithful continued with unusual calmness, "And finally, as to what Mr. Flatterer has testified, while avoiding those hateful words that I've been accused of using, I must still say that the prince of this town, all the rabble that he has appointed, his attendants, and those who were named by Mr. Flattery are more fit for being in Hell than in this town and country! And so, may the Lord have mercy on me!"

Then the judge addressed the jury, who were all watching and listening nearby. "Gentlemen of the jury," the judge said, leaning forward in his big chair, "you see this man before you who has been in the center of a great uproar in this town. You've also heard what these worthy gentlemen have testified against him, and you have heard his reply and confession. It lies now in your heartfelt decision as to whether he should live or die. However, before you decide, I think it's proper that I instruct you in the understanding of our law."

The judge sat back in his chair and began his explanation, as if telling his favorite story. "There was a decree made in the days of Pharaoh the Great, a servant to our king, that if those of a false religion should multiply and grow too strong for him, their males should be thrown into the river.[132]

"There was also a decree made in the days of Nebuchadnezzar the Great, another of his servants, that whoever would not fall down and worship his golden image should be thrown into a fiery furnace.[133]

"And yet another decree was made in the days of Darius that for a period of time, whoever called on any god other than him should be cast into the lion's den."[134]

The judge leveled his bony finger in the direction of Faithful and said, "Now this rebel has broken the substance of these laws, not only in thought, which is not an indictable offense, but also in word and action, which must not be tolerated.

"Concerning Pharaoh, his law was made with the assumption that it would prevent trouble even though no crime had yet been committed. But in this case, the evidence of a crime is apparent! With regard to the second and third precedents, you have witnessed how the prisoner argues

---

[132] Ex. 1:16
[133] Dan. 3:6
[134] Dan. 6:7

against our religion in much the same way. Therefore, for the treason that he has already confessed, he deserves to die as a criminal!"

Then the jury, whose names were Mr. Blindman, Mr. No-good, Mr. Malice, Mr. Love-lust, Mr. Live-loose, Mr. Heady, Mr. High-mind, Mr. Enmity, Mr. Liar, Mr. Cruelty, Mr. Hate-light, and Mr. Unforgiving, left the room in order to consider a verdict. Each jury member delivered their private verdict before the judge and unanimously concluded that Faithful was guilty.

Mr. Blindman, the foreman, wasted no time and said, "I clearly see that this man is a heretic!"

Then Mr. No-good added, "Let's be rid of this man off the face of the earth!"

"Yes!" said Mr. Malice, nodding his head in agreement. "I can't stand the very sight of him!"

"I could never tolerate him!" said Mr. Love-lust.

"Nor could I," said Mr. Live-loose, "because he was always condemning my lifestyle."

"Hang him! Hang him!" said Mr. Heady violently.

Mr. High-mind crossed his arms and said proudly, "He's a sorry good-for-nothing."

"My heart boils with anger against him!" said Mr. Enmity.

Mr. Liar confidently asserted, "He's a dishonest and unprincipled man."

"Hanging is too good for him!" said Mr. Cruelty.

"Let us get rid of him immediately!" said Mr. Hate-light.

Then Mr. Unforgiving said, "Even if I were to be given the whole world, I still could never be reconciled to him. Therefore, I say we deliver our verdict and find him guilty and deserving of death!"

And so they did.

Faithful was immediately condemned and returned to his cell, where he was to await the cruelest death that could be invented. Then they brought him out to execute him according to their law. First they whipped him, then they severely beat him, then they lanced his flesh with knives. After that, they stoned him then stabbed him with their swords. And last of all, they burned him to ashes at the stake. This is how Faithful died.

Now I noticed beyond the crowd a chariot and a team of horses waiting for Faithful. As soon as his enemies had killed him, he was taken up into the chariot and immediately carried up through the clouds with the sound of a trumpet. He was taken by the quickest route to the Celestial Gate.

But as for Christian, he had some time to rest and was sent back to prison, where he remained for some time. But He who overrules all things, having the power of their rage in His own hand, worked things out so that Christian had time to escape and could continue traveling on the Way.

As he left the town, he said, "Well, Faithful, you have faithfully professed your Lord, and so you will be blessed. When faithless ones, with all their worthless delights, are crying out under their hellish plights, sing, Faithful, sing, and let your name survive. For though they have killed you, yet you are alive!"

Chapter Eight

The Deceitfulness of Riches

After Christian escaped Vanity Fair, he did not journey alone. Eventually, he was joined by another pilgrim, named Hopeful, who was persuaded to become a pilgrim himself after witnessing the martyrdom of Christian and Faithful at the fair. So the two of them entered a brotherly covenant and committed to being companions for the journey. Just as one lost his life to bear testimony to the truth, another arose out of his ashes to become a companion for Christian. Hopeful also told Christian that there were many more from Vanity Fair who would be following after them.

Not long after leaving the fair, they caught up with a man walking ahead of them named Mr. By-Ends. They said to him, "What country are you from, and why are you traveling in this direction?"

"I'm from the town of Fair-Speech, and I'm heading to the Celestial City," the man responded, although he did not mention his name.

"From Fair-Speech, you say?" Christian inquired, cocking his head to one side. "Are there any godly people who live there?"[135]

"Yes," he responded confidently, "I certainly hope so!"

---

[135] Prov. 26:25

"Please, sir, tell us your name." Christian asked again.

"We don't know each other, but if you're going my way, I would enjoy your company. If not, I'm satisfied to just travel alone."

Christian sidestepped the question because he wanted to learn more about this man. "I've heard of this town of Fair-Speech, and if I remember correctly, it's a wealthy place."

"Yes, I can guarantee you that much!" the man said enthusiastically. "In fact, I have many rich friends and family there."

"Then, if I may be so bold, who are some of these friends and family?"

"Almost the whole town!" he said confidently. "In particular, there's Lord Turn-About, Lord Time-Server, and Lord Fair-Speech, whose ancestors the town is named after. Also, there's Mr. Smooth-Man, Mr. Facing-Both-Ways, Mr. Anything, and the pastor of the church, Mr. Two-Tongues, who is my mother's brother.

"To tell you the truth, I have become a gentleman of high standing even though my great-grandfather was nothing but a waterman for hire who would look one way and row another. I got most of my estate by the same occupation."

"Are you a married man?" asked Christian.

"Yes," he replied. "My wife is a very virtuous woman and the daughter of Madam Pretender, also a virtuous woman. So, as you can imagine, she comes from a very honorable family with a high level of breeding. She knows how to behave toward all kinds of people, whether princes or peasants. It's true that our religion differs from those of the stricter sort but only in two small points.

"First, our religion is calm and comfortable; in other words, we never strive against the wind and tide. Secondly, we are passionate about religion that is fashionable and favorable. We love to parade our faith in front of others when things are going well and receive their praise."

Believing he had gathered the information he needed, Christian pulled Hopeful to the side and said, "I believe this man is Mr. By-Ends of Fair-Speech. If this is true, we have quite a scoundrel in our company, the likes of which is often found in these parts."

Hopeful looked at Christian a little surprised then suggested, "You should ask him. I wouldn't think that he'd be ashamed of his name."

Christian approached the man again and said, "Sir, you talk as if you know everything in the whole world. If I'm correct, and I believe that I am, isn't your name Mr. By-Ends of Fair-speech?"

"That's not my name!" By-Ends quickly retorted. "It's just a nickname given to me by those who can't stand me." He paused for a moment, calmed his voice, and then said, "It disappoints me to have to tolerate that abusive name, in much the same way that other good men have been similarly maligned."

Christian continued to pursue his line of questioning. "But have your actions ever provided a reason for these men to correctly call you by this name?"

"Never, never!" said By-Ends angrily. "The worst that I've ever done that might give them a reason to call me this name was having the good fortune to make the most profitable decision at just the right time. But if I'm criticized for being profitable, which was certainly by chance, then I will choose to count my gain as a blessing rather than accept the hatred and disapproval from such men."

But Christian was not convinced. "I was so sure that you were the man that I had heard about, and to be honest, I fear that this name belongs to you more appropriately than you are willing to admit."

"Well, you may think what you like. I cannot help that," By-Ends remarked, brushing off Christian's assertion. "You'll find me a good traveling companion, that is, if you allow me to go with you."

Christian immediately stopped walking and spoke directly to By-Ends. "If you're to walk with us, you must go against the wind and tide, which, as I understand, is against your convictions. You must also welcome religion in all its rags as well as when it's fashionable and favorable and stand by the faithful who are bound in chains as well as when they walk in the streets with praise."

By-Ends angrily snapped back, "You should not impose your beliefs on me or put pressure on my faith but rather respect my freedom and let me travel with you."

Christian held up his hand. "Not a step further, unless you agree to what I've proposed."

By-Ends shook his head. "I'll never desert my longstanding principles, since they are harmless and profitable. If I'm not allowed to travel with you, I'll just continue as I did before we met and travel alone, that is, unless someone else overtakes me and appreciates my company."

Now I saw in my dream that Christian and Hopeful left By-Ends and kept their distance by moving ahead of him. But one of them looked back and saw three men following him named Mr. Hold-the-World, Mr. Money-Love, and Mr. Save-All. They all caught up with By-Ends and greeted one another.

By-Ends was familiar with all three men as they had formerly been school friends taught by a certain Mr. Gripe-man, a teacher in Love-gain, which was a northern market town in Coveting County. This teacher taught them the art of prospering by accruing possessions by violence, cheating, flattering, lying, and fake religion. These four classmates learned so much of the art from their master that all were capable of running such a school themselves.

Mr. Money-Love pointed at Christian and Hopeful for they were still in view. "Who's that walking on the road ahead of us?"

"They are a couple of men from a distant country who are going on a pilgrimage in their own strange way," said By-Ends.

"Really!" said Mr. Money-Love. "Then why didn't they stay so that we could enjoy each other's company? It seems as though we're all traveling in the same direction."

"It *would* seem so," said By-Ends sarcastically, "but those two men are so rigid and in love with their own ideas that they do not value the opinions of others. Even a godly man who does not agree with them in everything is immediately dismissed from their company."

"That's too bad," said Mr. Save-All, joining the conversation. "We've read about people like this who consider themselves overly righteous and rigid, which eventually leads to judging and condemning everyone but themselves. So tell me, in what ways were you different than them?"

By-Ends wasted no time in sharing his opinion of Christian and Hopeful. "Why, according to their arrogant behavior, they believe it's their duty to rush ahead on their journey in all types of weather, while I'm in favor of waiting for the right wind and tide. They're for risking it all for God, and in an instant, I would grasp every advantage to secure my life and property. They're for holding on to their beliefs even though all other men oppose them, but I'm for religion that's tolerant of the times and not a threat to my safety. They're for religion when it dresses in rags and is considered contemptible, but I'm for parading my faith in front of others when things are going well and receiving praise."

"Yes, and hold on to your beliefs, my good Mr. By-Ends," said Mr. Hold-the-World. "As for me, I can only count him a fool who has the freedom to keep what he has but then is so unwise as to lose it. Instead, let us be wise as serpents. It's best to make hay while the sun shines. You see how the bee lies still in winter and wakes herself only for profit and pleasure. Sometimes God sends rain and at other times sunshine. If those two are foolish enough to walk through the rain, let us be content to take the fair weather for us.

"As for me, I like a religion best that enjoys the security of God's good blessings poured out on us. When you think about it, it stands to reason that if God has given us the good things of this life, then He would want us to continue to enjoy them in this life for His sake. Abraham and Solomon grew rich through religion, and Job says that a good man will store up gold as dust. But the men you've described in front of us sound nothing like this."

"I think that we're all in agreement on this matter, so there's no need to discuss it anymore," said Mr. Save-All.

"No, nothing more needs to be said," said Mr. Money-Love, "because if a man will not believe Scripture or reason—and it's evident that we have both on our side—he will not appreciate his own freedom or care for his own safety."

"My brothers," said By-Ends, changing the subject, "since we're all going on the same journey, and to distract us from thinking about bad things, let me ask you this question. Suppose a man who is a minister, or a businessman, or some other profession is presented with an opportunity for promotion. But let's say that the only way that he can get this promotion is by becoming extremely passionate about certain aspects of religion that he previously neglected. Can he not use this religious means to attain his promotion and still remain a perfectly honest man?"

"I believe I understand the basis of your question," said Mr.

Money-Love, "and with everyone's permission, I will attempt to provide you an answer."

Seeing no objection from his fellow travelers, Money-Love continued, "First, let's examine your question as it concerns the minister. Suppose a minister, a reputable man, is pastoring a small church on a meager salary, yet he has his eye on a greater, more prestigious and prosperous church. Now let's suppose he has an opportunity to get appointed to this prosperous church if he studies more and preaches more frequently and passionately. However, he finds that he must also alter some of his principles because the people at this new church expect it. For my part, I see no reason why he should not do this, provided the church has called him. In fact, there are several other reasons besides this why he should seek this career advancement, provided he's an honest man."

Money-Love paused to gather his thoughts then continued, "First, it's not sinful to desire more pay, and since the opportunity has come his way, it must be in the providence of God for him to pursue it. So he should pursue this opportunity with all his might without questioning his conscience.

"Secondly, his desire for the more prosperous church makes him study more and become a more passionate preacher and, as a result, a better man. Indeed, he can improve his mind and natural abilities, which is certainly according to God's will.

"Thirdly, compromising some of his principles in order to comply with the expectations of the new church so that he may better serve them is not wrong. If anything, it indicates that he's capable of practicing self-denial with a sweet and winning attitude, affirming that he has the qualities that will allow him to excel in the ministry.

"And finally, a minister who leaves a small church for a large church is evidence of success and should not in any way be judged as covetous. Rather, he should be considered as one who is working to improve both himself and his career for the benefit of his call and the opportunity to do good work.

"Now, to the second part of your question, concerning the businessman you mentioned. Suppose this businessman has an unprofitable business but finds that he can expand his market and tap into an even larger customer base and perhaps even find a wealthy woman to be his wife. All he needs to do is join a local church and become religious while gaining the confidence and trust of the church members. Again, as far as I can see, there's no reason why he should not pursue this course. And here's why:

"First, it's always good to go to church and engage in religion, regardless of the motivation.

"Secondly, it's not sinful to marry a wealthy woman or, for that matter, to convince more customers from the church to come into his business.

"Finally, since being religious is good, getting a wife is good, and growing your business is good, then getting all of this by being religious must certainly be good. So to become religious in order to get all these is a good and profitable pursuit."

They all enthusiastically applauded Mr. Money-Love's answer to By-Ends' question, agreeing that it was sensible and worthwhile. And since they were convinced that no one could possibly contradict this argument, and because Christian and Hopeful, who had earlier opposed Mr. By-Ends, were still within calling distance, they devised a plan to challenge them with the question as soon as they could catch up.

Without hesitation, they immediately called ahead to Christian and Hopeful, who waited until the four men could catch up. However, on their way, they mutually agreed that Mr. Hold-the-World would be the spokesperson rather than By-Ends to avoid rekindling the previous heated discussion he had had with the two pilgrims.

After catching up to Christian and Hopeful and a short round of greetings, Hold-the-World presented the question to them and arrogantly asked them to answer if they could.

"Even someone new to the faith could answer ten thousand such questions," Christian said without hesitation. "According to John 6:26, it's unlawful to follow Christ for what you think you will get out of it. How much more detestable is it then to use Him for temporary advantage in order to obtain and enjoy the world! The only ones who believe this are heathens, hypocrites, devils, and sorcerers.

"As for the heathens, when Hamor and Shechem wanted the daughters and cattle of Jacob, they realized that the only way to do so was by being circumcised. So they said to their companions, 'If every male of ours is circumcised, as they are circumcised, won't their cattle, possessions, and every beast they own be ours?' The daughters and cattle of Jacob were what they wanted, and their religious profession became the tool they used to obtain it. You can read the whole story in Genesis 34:20–24.

"Now, the hypocritical Pharisees were also of this belief. Their long prayers were all for show, while they defrauded widows out of their homes. For this reason, God will punish them severely. You can read about this in Luke 20:46–47.

"Judas the devil was of this belief as well. He desired the disciples' money bag and its contents, but he was lost, cast away, and the very one doomed to destruction.[136]

"Simon the sorcerer was of this belief too. He wanted the power of the Holy Spirit so that he might obtain wealth, but Peter chastised him and told him to repent, according to Acts 8:19–22.

"Neither does it escape my attention that the man who takes up religion for worldly gain will throw away religion for

---

[136] John 12:6

worldly gain. Just as Judas desired religion for worldly gain, he quickly sold it and his Master for the same reason. So then, to claim that it's right to use religion to gain the world, as I believe you have done, is wrong, irreligious, hypocritical, and devilish, and the only reward you'll receive will be according to your own works."

The four men just stood staring at each other without knowing what to say to Christian. Hopeful approved of the soundness of Christian's answer, so there was a heavy silence between them. Eventually, By-Ends and his companions staggered behind them, hoping that Christian and Hopeful might outpace them.

Christian said to Hopeful, "If these men cannot stand before the sentence of men, what will they do with the sentence of God? And if they don't know how to answer and are speechless when dealt with by mere men, what will they do when they are rebuked by the flames of a devouring fire?"

The Snare of the Silver Mine

Christian and Hopeful once again walked ahead of By-Ends and his friends until they came to a pleasant meadow called Ease, which they traveled across quite comfortably. However, the plain was so narrow that they quickly crossed it and reached the other side.

Now, at the far side of the plain was a little hill called Lucre, also called Greedy Profit. In that hill was a rare silver mine that other passing pilgrims had turned aside to investigate. However, some were killed when they got too close to the edge of the mine shaft and the unstable ground beneath them broke. Others were severely injured and could not, to their dying day, be recovered.

Then I saw in my dream that a short distance off the Way, near the silver mine, stood a man named Demas, who was inviting passing pilgrims to stop and see. He said to Christian and Hopeful, "Hello, friends! Come on over here, and I'll show you something amazing!"

"What could be so deserving of our attention that it would cause us to turn from the Way to see it?" Christian called back.

"It's a silver mine and full of treasure for those who will dig," he replied, motioning toward the mine. "If you'll come, with only a little effort, you may become very wealthy."

Hopeful said excitedly, "Let's go check this out!"

"Not me!" said Christian, shaking his head. "I've heard

about the reputation of this mine and the number of lives it has destroyed. Besides, the treasure is nothing but a snare to those who seek it because it hinders them in their pilgrimage."

Christian then called out to Demas, "Isn't this place dangerous? Has it not hindered many in their pilgrimage?"[137]

"It's not very dangerous," said Demas, blushing as he spoke. "It's only dangerous for those that are careless."

Christian turned to Hopeful and said, "Let's not waste any time, but instead, let's keep true to our path."

Hopeful agreed. "I guarantee you that when By-Ends arrives here, if he receives the same invitation that we have, he will definitely go to the mines to get a closer look."

Christian nodded. "I have no doubt that he will since his principles lead him in that direction. A hundred to one he dies there!"

But Demas was persistent and called to them again, "But will you not come over and just take a closer look?"

Then Christian answered bluntly, saying, "Demas, you are an enemy to those who are pursuing the right ways of the Lord of this Way. I know you've already been condemned by one of His Majesty's judges for turning aside yourself.[138] Why do you want to bring us to the same condemnation as you? Besides, if we all turn aside here, our Lord the King would certainly hear about this and reveal our shame. Our desire is to stand with boldness before Him."

Demas pleaded further, "I'm also a pilgrim, just like you. If you'll wait just a little bit, I would like to walk with you."

"What's your name?" Christian asked. "Is it not Demas? For that's the name that I've been calling you."

"Yes, my name is Demas," he said. "I'm Abraham's son."

---

[137] Hosea 9:6
[138] 2 Tim. 4:10

"I know you. Gehazi was your great-grandfather and Judas your father, and it seems you have followed in their footsteps. What you are suggesting is nothing more than a devilish trick. Your father was hanged as a traitor, and you deserve no better reward.[139] You can be assured that when we come before the King, we will tell Him of your behavior."

Christian and Hopeful continued on the way just as By-Ends and his friends were coming within sight. As soon as Demas invited them to look at the mines, they eagerly accepted, turned, and went over to him. Now, whether they fell into the mine shaft by looking over the edge, or whether they went down to dig, or whether they were smothered at the bottom by the poisonous fumes that often occurred there, I do not know. But I do know that they were never seen on the Way again.

Christian said, "By-Ends and silver Demas are one and the same. When one calls, the other runs so that he may share in his profit. So even though these two may do well in this world, they will go no further."

---

[139] 2 Kings 5:20–27; Matt. 26:14–15, 27:3–5

A Monumental Warning

No sooner had Christian and Hopeful crossed the Plain of Ease than they encountered a strange and unmistakable sight right next to the highway. Both men were concerned because it appeared to be the shape of a woman who had been transformed into a pillar. They stood staring at it for some time, puzzled by its meaning.

After a while, Hopeful noticed an inscription written in unusual handwriting above the monument. Being no scholar, he called Christian, who was more educated, to interpret the meaning. After Christian examined and studied the writing, he found the meaning to be "Remember Lot's Wife!"

He read it to Hopeful, and they both agreed that it was Lot's wife, who was turned into a pillar of salt when she looked back with a covetous heart while fleeing Sodom for safety.[140] This amazing experience made the two pilgrims stop and think.

"Ah, brother," Christian said, "this is truly a timely warning for us to find this pillar coming just after Demas's invitation to view the mine at Lucre. Had we gone over, as he wanted us to—and as you were first inclined to do—it's very likely that we would have become a pillar like this woman, a similar spectacle for those that would follow after us to see."

"I'm sorry I was so foolish," Hopeful said, feeling the weight of his mistake. "It's a wonder that I'm not a pillar of

---

[140] Gen. 19:26

salt just like Lot's wife! What was the difference between her sin and mine? She only looked back, but I had an actual desire to go in and see the mine! Let grace be honored here, and let me be ashamed that my heart ever considered such a thought."

"Let's talk about what we've learned to help us remember in the future," Christian said, gesturing at the monument. "This woman did not suffer in the destruction of Sodom, so she escaped that judgment. Yet as is evident here, she was destroyed by another judgment and turned into this pillar of salt."

"This is true," Hopeful responded. "May she serve as both a warning and an example—a warning in that we should avoid her sin and an example of the judgment we will experience if we do not heed this warning, just like Korah, Dathan, and Abiram, with the two hundred fifty men who perished in their sin, were also examples to others to beware."[141]

Hopeful paused for a moment and then said thoughtfully, "But above all, I'm curious about one thing. How is it that Demas and his friends can so confidently walk over there looking for treasure while this woman just looked behind her and was turned into a pillar of salt? Scripture does not record her taking one step in the wrong direction, yet her punishment made her a visible example to all those digging in the mine. The fact is, if they would just look up, they would see her!"

Christian thought about what Hopeful had said. "It's an amazing thing to consider, and it indicates that Demas and his friends' hearts have grown desperate for the things of this world. I cannot decide who they would more accurately be compared to—those that pick pockets in the presence of the judge or those that steal purses under the gallows.

"Scripture tells us that the men of Sodom were exceptionally sinful because they were sinners in the sight of

---

141 Numbers 16:31–32, 26:9–10

the Lord. In other words, they openly sinned before Him, not considering the kindness He had shown by providing them the land of Sodom, which was like the Garden of Eden before the Fall.[142]

"Therefore, this provoked the Lord even more to jealousy and made their judgment as hot as the fire of the Lord of Heaven could make it. So it's reasonable to conclude that those, such as we have been talking about, that sin in the sight of God despite His many warnings set before them must be severely judged."

"I have no doubt what you said is true," Hopeful said. "But how merciful it is that neither you but especially I have not also been made an example! This occasion gives us the opportunity to thank God, to fear Him, and to always remember Lot's wife."

---

[142] Gen. 13:10–13

Chapter Nine
Taking the Easy Path

Then I saw that the pilgrims went on their way toward a pleasant river that King David called the River of God but John called the River of the Water of Life.[143] They were delighted to find the Way following the bank of the river, and they drank from it to refresh their weary spirits.

On both sides of the river bank stood green trees with all kinds of fruit, and they ate the leaves to prevent sickness as well as to provide other medicinal benefits. There were also beautifully adorned meadows full of lilies on both sides of the river, and it was green all year long. Feeling safe, they laid down in the meadow to sleep. When they woke, they gathered fruit from the trees and drank from the river once again then laid back down to sleep. This continued for several days and nights, and then they sang:

> *Look how these Crystal Streams do glide*
> *To comfort pilgrims by the highway side*
> *The green meadows with their fragrant smell*
> *Produce dainties for them, and who can tell*
> *What pleasant fruit and leaves these trees do yield*

---

[143] Ps. 65:9, Rev. 22:1, Ezek. 7:1–9

Will soon sell all, that he may buy this field.

When they were ready to resume their journey, since they were not yet at the end, they ate, drank, and then left.

Before they had gone too far, the river and the Way split off from each other in different directions. They were saddened but dared not venture off the Way even though the path became rough and their feet were sore from walking. But it wasn't long before they became weary and discouraged[144] and longed for an easier path.

A little ahead of them, on the left side of the road, there was a set of steps built over a fence that bordered a meadow, which was called By-Path Meadow.

Christian said to Hopeful, "If this meadow runs alongside the Way, let's cross over into it." He hurried over to the steps to investigate and, sure enough, found a path on the other side of the fence that seemed to run parallel to their own.

"This is exactly what I was hoping for!" said Christian excitedly, pointing over the steps. "This path will be much easier. Come on, Hopeful, let's cross over."

Hopeful was hesitant and replied, "But how do we know this path will not lead us off the Way?"

"That's not likely," said Christian, beginning to climb over the steps. "Look! This path is parallel to ours and only on the other side of the fence."

Hopeful was soon persuaded by Christian to follow him over the steps. Together they traveled the new path, finding it much easier on their feet. They had not traveled too far when they spotted a man walking on the path in front of them whose name was Vain-Confidence. They called out to him and asked him where this path led.

---

[144] Num. 21:4

"To the Celestial Gate!" he replied.

"See!" said Christian, smiling confidently at Hopeful. "Didn't I tell you so? This just confirms that we are heading in the right direction."

They began to follow Vain-Confidence, but as night came and it grew very dark, they lost sight of him. It was so dark that Vain-Confidence could not see the path in front of him and fell into a deep pit. This pit was a trap specially prepared by the king of those grounds to catch vainglorious fools. When he fell in, his body was broken into pieces.[145]

Christian and Hopeful heard Vain-Confidence fall and called out to see how he was doing, but there was no reply. They only heard someone groaning.

"Where are we now?" asked Hopeful, visibly concerned.

Christian stayed silent with the fearful realization that he had led Hopeful off the Way and into danger. Suddenly it began to rain, thunder, and lighting in a most dreadful manner. The rain came down in streams and began to flood the path.

Hopeful groaned inwardly and said, "Oh, if only I had stayed on the Way!"

"Who would have thought this path would have led us off the Way?" Christian asked as his confidence was beginning to quickly fade.

"I had my fears from the very beginning and expressed those to you with a gentle warning," Hopeful said, obviously irritated. "Perhaps I should have been clearer, but you are more mature in the faith than I."

"You are such a good friend. Please do not be offended," said Christian with sorrow in his voice. "I'm so sorry that I led you off the Way and exposed you to imminent danger. Please forgive me, Hopeful, as I did not act with evil intent."

---

[145] Is. 9:16

Hopeful warmly placed his hand on Christian's shoulder, even as they were now becoming soaked from the rain. "Say no more. I forgive you and have no doubt this will be for our good."

"I'm so glad to have a merciful companion with me." Christian then immediately turned his attention to the matter at hand. "Let's not stand here any longer, as we are in danger. Let's try to go back to the steps right away."

"In that case, I'll lead the way," said Hopeful as he started to turn back.

"No," said Christian grabbing Hopeful's arm. "Please let me go first. Then if we encounter danger, I will be the first to deal with it since it's my fault for leading us off the Way."

"Absolutely not," said Hopeful, raising his voice to be heard over the rain and thunder. "Your leading us would not be a good idea since your mind is still troubled and might lead us farther off the Way."

Then they heard an encouraging voice saying, "Let your heart be toward the highway, even the Way that you formerly went. Turn and go back again."[146]

But by this time the floodwaters had risen much higher, making traveling back to the Way very dangerous. It was then that I understood that it's easier to leave the Way when you are on it than it is to get back onto it. Still, they made every effort to return. But it was so dark and the floodwaters had risen so high that they nearly drowned nine or ten times trying to return.

Even with all their skill and determination, they were unable to make it back to the steps that night. Eventually they found refuge under a small shelter and sat down awaiting daybreak, but being exhausted, they fell asleep.

---

[146] Jer. 31:21

Trapped in Doubting Castle

Not far from the place where they were lying, there was a castle called Doubting Castle. Giant Despair, the owner of the castle, got up early the next morning to walk up and down his fields and found Christian and Hopeful asleep on his property.

The pilgrims were rudely awakened by the gruff and brutal giant demanding, "Where are you from, and what are you doing on my property?"

They explained that they were pilgrims who had lost their way.

"You're trespassing and have no right to trample upon and sleep on my property! You must come with me right now!" he said, forcing them to go along with him. They had very little choice given that he was bigger and stronger, and they could say very little as they knew they were at fault.

The giant drove his prisoners like cattle all the way to his castle and locked them up in a very dark dungeon cell. Christian and Hopeful's spirits soon became discouraged in the smelly and nasty cell. They laid there from Wednesday morning until Saturday night without any food, water, light, or even someone to ask how they were doing. The dungeon was a sinister place, far from any friends or family.[147] It wasn't long before Christian became depressed, knowing it was his

---

[147] Ps. 88:18

hasty advice that got them into this mess.

Giant Despair had a wife named Diffidence. As he was going to bed that evening, he told her about what he had done, explaining how he had taken a couple of prisoners and thrown them into his dungeon for trespassing on his property. "What do you think I should do with them?" he asked his wife while getting into bed.

Diffidence was very curious about these new prisoners and asked, "Tell me more about them. Who are they? Where did they come from, and where are they going?"

The giant told her everything he knew. Already Diffidence did not trust the likes of Christian and Hopeful and quickly offered advice. "Tomorrow you should go down to their cell and beat them without mercy!"

When he got up the next morning, he grabbed a short, heavy club and went down into the dungeon and began to beat them like dogs, even though they showed him no disrespect. His attacks were so severe that they could not protect themselves or escape. Once he had finished, the giant left them there for the rest of the day to grieve and mourn in pain.

That night, Diffidence talked with her husband once again about the prisoners and discovered they were still alive. This time, she advised him to recommend suicide to Christian and Hopeful.

The next morning, the giant went to the dungeon in the same surly manner as before and noticed how sore they were from the beatings he had given them yesterday. "Since neither of you are very likely to ever leave this dungeon, your best alternative is to kill yourself! You can use a knife, a noose, or poison," he said, laying those items down in the cage. "Why would you choose to go on living seeing that your life is filled with so much sorrow?"

They begged him to let them go, which only made the giant

furious, and he rushed to kill them. Undoubtedly, he would have succeeded except he fell into one of his seizures, which often happened on a sunny day. During these fits, his hands became temporarily paralyzed, so he left them alone to consider his advice with the tools he had provided.

Christian and Hopeful began an intense discussion about whether they should take their own lives, as the giant had suggested.

"Hopeful," said Christian, visibly distraught and rubbing his sore head, "what should we do? This is a miserable life to live. As for me, I don't know whether it's better to live like this or die by my own hand. My soul chooses strangling rather than living, and the grave seems a more desirable place than this dungeon."[148]

He paused for a moment, lowered his voice, and said, "What do you think? Should we take the giant's advice?"

In pain, Hopeful eased his back against the cell wall for support as he sat down. "It's true that our present condition is horrible, and I would welcome death rather than live in this misery forever. But don't forget what the Lord of the country where we are heading has said: 'Do not murder.' This includes another person or by taking the giant's advice and killing ourselves. Besides, when you murder someone, you can only commit murder of that person's body, but to kill yourself is to kill the body and soul at the same time."

Hopeful could tell he was starting to get through to Christian and continued. "And beyond that, since you're talking of an easy grave, have you forgotten that Hell is reserved for murderers? For no murderer has eternal life. And let's also remember that Giant Despair does not have control over the law of our Lord. It's my understanding that there have been others like us that have been captured by him and yet escaped."

---

[148] Job 7:15

Writing in pain, he slowly turned himself and faced Christian. "Who knows. Perhaps the God who made the world may cause Giant Despair to die. Or at some time or another, he may forget to lock us in. Or sooner or later, he might have another paralyzing seizure while he is with us and lose the use of his hands. I can guarantee you that if it happens again, I will muster up enough courage to try my hardest to escape. I was a fool to have not tried it earlier. However, my brother, let's be patient and continue to endure. Perhaps a happy release is in our future! But let's not be our own murderers."

Hopeful's words helped ease Christian's mind as they continued together in the dark that day, depressed and in pain.

As evening approached, the giant went down to the dungeon to see if Christian and Hopeful had taken his advice. He found them alive but barely so as they were malnourished and beaten so badly with severe wounds that they could hardly breathe. But, as I said, he found them alive and fell into a furious rage.

"Seeing that you have disobeyed my advice, it will now be worse for you than had you never been born!" The giant was seething as he left, slamming the cell door behind him.

Instantly, they were filled with fear, and I think Christian fainted. But after coming to, they continued to discuss whether it was best for them to take the giant's advice and end their lives. Once again, Christian was tempted to do so.

"Christian, do you not remember how brave you were before?" said Hopeful, doing his best to encourage him. "Apollyon could not hurt you and neither could all that you heard, saw, or felt in the Valley of the Shadow of Death! Look at all the hardship, terror, and grief you've already experienced. Are you now nothing but fear? Remember that I, too, am in this dungeon with you and a far weaker man than you. This giant has wounded both of us and has deprived me also of any food, water, or light.

"But still, let's exercise a little more patience," persuaded Hopeful. "Remember how courageous you were at Vanity Fair? You were not afraid of the chains, the cage, or even a bloody death! Let's persevere with patience just as long as we can, at least to avoid the shame that isn't suitable for a Christian to be found in."

Later that night, the giant and his wife were in bed, and she asked him, "Did the prisoners take your advice today and commit suicide?"

"No! They are strong scoundrels," he said angrily as he could not seem to break their spirits. "They would choose to stand firm under hardships rather than to take their own lives."

Diffidence was beginning to think she would never be rid of Christian and Hopeful and said, "Take them into the castle yard tomorrow, and show them the bones and skulls of those that you've already killed. Then make them believe that the same will happen to them by the end of the week."

When morning came, the giant took Christian and Hopeful to the castle yard and showed them the remains of other pilgrims, as his wife had suggested. "These were pilgrims like you once," he said, making a broad gesture to the castle yard. "They also trespassed on my property as you did. When I saw fit, I tore them to pieces, and within ten days, I'll do the same to you! Now go! Get back down to your cell again!"

He beat them all the way back to the dungeon, and they lay all day on Saturday in the same miserable condition as before.

Night came, and Diffidence and her husband were once again talking about their prisoners. The old giant was amazed that neither his beatings nor his counsel that they should take their own lives had worked.

Diffidence began to feel uneasy. "I fear they live in hope of being rescued or have hidden tools on them to pick the locks and will escape."

"You think so, my dear?" the giant said curiously. "In that case, I will search them in the morning."

On Saturday, around midnight, Christian and Hopeful began to pray and continued praying until morning had nearly come.

Now, a little before dawn, Christian had a sudden revelation and became very excited. "What a fool I am, Hopeful. I've been lying in this stinking dungeon when I could have just as well walked free! I have a key in my pocket next to my heart called Promise that I'm sure will open any lock in Doubting Castle."

Hopeful could not believe what he was hearing. "That's good news, Christian! Pull it out of your pocket, and try it right now!"

Christian took the key and began to try the lock of the dungeon door, whose bolt, as he turned the key, sprang back easily. The cell door flew wide open, freeing Christian and Hopeful.

Next they made their way to the castle yard door, and his key easily opened that door as well. Eventually they arrived at the iron gate, which also had to be opened for them to escape. Christian found that lock a little harder to turn, but when it finally did, they threw open the gates and quickly escaped. However, the hinges made such a loud creaking sound that it woke Giant Despair, who jumped out of bed to pursue his prisoners. As he did, he fell into another one of his seizures, making it impossible for him to chase them.

After escaping, Christian and Hopeful made it back to the King's highway, where they were safe once again and out of the giant's jurisdiction.

Once they had returned over the steps at the fence, they began to discuss what should be done at those steps to prevent others that would come after them from falling into the hands of Giant Despair. They agreed to erect a sign with clear instructions written on it saying, "Over these steps is the way to Doubting Castle whose lord is Giant Despair and who despises the King of the Celestial Country and seeks to kill all who go there." As a result, many pilgrims that came after them read the sign and escaped the danger.

Afterward, they sang:

Out of the way we went, and then we found
What was to tread upon forbidden ground:
And let them that come after have a care,
Lest heedlessness makes them as we to fare;
Lest they, for trespassing, his prisoners are,
Whose castle's Doubting, and whose name's Despair.

Chapter Ten

The Shepherds in the Mountains

After Christian and Hopeful escaped Doubting Castle, they continued on the Way, ascending the Delectable Mountains that belonged to the King, which I previously mentioned before. There they found gardens, orchards, vineyards, and fountains, where they washed themselves and were refreshed and nourished.

There were shepherds on top of these mountains feeding their flocks and standing by the side of the Way. It was customary in those days for weary travelers to stop and talk, so the pilgrims approached the shepherds who were leaning on their staffs, and asked, "Who owns these Delectable Mountains and the sheep grazing on them?"

The shepherds replied, "The mountains belong to Emmanuel, and from here you can see the Celestial City. The sheep are also His, and He laid down His life for them."[149]

"So this is the way to the Celestial City?" Christian asked excitedly.

They nodded and said, "You're going in the right direction."

Christian gazed down the road. "How much farther do we have to go?"

---

[149] John 10:11–15

"It's too far for any except those that will no doubt arrive there."

Christian glanced over at Hopeful and then back to the shepherds. "Is the way ahead safe or dangerous?"

"It's safe for some, but sinful men will fall there."[150]

Christian and Hopeful were completely exhausted from their journey. "We are very tired. Is there a place where we might be able to rest awhile?"

"The Lord of these mountains has ordered us not to forget to entertain strangers," said the shepherds.[151] "Therefore, everything that's good here is for your refreshment."

When the shepherds learned that Christian and Hopeful had been traveling on the Way, they began to ask them many of the same questions that had been asked before in other places, including, "Where did you come from?", "How did you enter the Way?", and "How have you persevered this far?" The shepherds knew that very few pilgrims that began a journey to these mountains would ever show their face here. After Christian and Hopeful told their story, the shepherds invited them to stay, saying, "Welcome to the Delectable Mountains!"

The shepherds, whose names were Knowledge, Experience, Watchful, and Sincere, led them by the hand to their tents, where they ate a meal that was prepared for them. In addition, the shepherds said, "We would like for you to stay here awhile and spend some time with us while enjoying the comforts of the Delectable Mountains." Christian and Hopeful agreed to stay, and since it was late, they all went to bed.

The next morning, at the shepherds' invitation, Christian and Hopeful walked with them on the mountains for a while, enjoying a pleasant view from every side.

---

[150] Hos. 14:9
[151] Heb. 13:2

The shepherds began to talk among themselves, saying, "Should we show them the wonders found only in these mountains?" They all agreed to do so and then led Christian and Hopeful to the top of a hill called Error, which was very steep on the farthest side. "Look down to the bottom," they said.

When Christian and Hopeful peered over, they saw several men at the bottom who were torn in pieces, having obviously fallen from the top.

"What does this mean?" Christian asked, unable to remove his eyes from the carnage below.

The shepherds answered, "Haven't you heard about the people who were led into error by listening to Hymenius and Philetus with regard to the faith of the resurrection of the body?"[152]

"Yes," they answered.

"That's who you see at the bottom of this mountain, and they have remained unburied to this day," the shepherds said. "They have now become a warning for others to be careful how high they climb or how close they come to the extreme edge of this mountain."

The shepherds then led them to the top of another mountain, named Caution, and told them to look far off into the valley, in the direction that they came. When they did, they thought they could see several men walking up and down among several graves there. It was obvious that these men were blind because they were stumbling over the graves, unable to find their way out.

Christian asked once again, "What does this mean?"

The shepherds answered, "Before you came to these mountains, did you notice a step leading over into a meadow

---

[152] 2 Tim. 2:17–18

on the left-hand side of the Way?"

Christian and Hopeful regretfully remembered the dark castle from which they had just escaped and sheepishly replied, "Yes."

"From those steps," said the shepherds, "there's a path leading directly to Doubting Castle, which is owned by Giant Despair." They pointed to the blind wandering among the graves. "These men were once on a journey, just as you are now, that is, until they came to that step. You see, the right Way was rough in that area, so they chose to leave the Way and cross over into the meadow and were taken captive by Giant Despair and cast into Doubting Castle.

"After they had been kept in the dungeon for some time, the giant eventually blinded them and led them among those graves, where he has left them to wander to this very day so that the saying of the wise man might be fulfilled: 'He that wanders out of the Way of understanding will remain in the congregation of the dead.'"[153]

After hearing this, Christian and Hopeful looked at each other with tears streaming down their faces but said nothing to the shepherds.

The shepherds continued guiding them to another place in the valley, where there was a door on the side of a hill. Opening the door, they told them to look in.

The pilgrims looked inside and found it very dark and smoky. They also thought they heard the rumbling sounds of a fire, the cries of tormented souls, and the stench of sulfur in the air.

Christian was terrified and turned back to the shepherds with his voice quivering. "What does this mean?"

The shepherds told them, "This is a road to Hell, where

---

[153] Prov. 21:16

hypocrites enter—those like Esau, who would sell his birthright; Judas, who would sell his Master; Alexander, who would blaspheme the gospel; or Ananias and his wife Sapphira, who would lie and deceive."

Hopeful thought for a moment then asked, "Is it true that each of them had the reputation of being a pilgrim like us?"

The Shepherds responded, "Yes, and they traveled quite a distance too."

"Exactly how far did these pilgrims travel before they were miserably cast away?" Hopeful asked.

"Some completed most of the journey," responded the Shepherds, "while others did not make it so far as these mountains."

Christian and Hopeful said to one another, "We need to cry to the Strong for strength."

"Yes! And you will also have need to draw on that strength when you have it," said the shepherds.

By this time, the pilgrims had a desire to press on, and the shepherds agreed that they should. So they walked together toward the end of the mountains.

The Shepherds said to one another, "Let's show them a view of the gates of the Celestial City, provided they have the skill to look through our perspective glass."

The pilgrims were excited at the prospect and were led to the top of a high hill called Clear and given the shepherds' perspective glass to look through.

They tried to look through it, but it was difficult to hold the perspective glass steady because they were still shaking due to the memory of the previous sight. Still, they thought they saw something like a gate and some of the glory of the place.

Then they went away, and sang,

Thus, by the shepherds, secrets are revealed,
Which from all other men are kept concealed.
Come to the shepherds then, if you would see
Things deep, things hid, and that mysterious be.

When they were about to leave, one of the shepherds gave them written instructions describing the Way ahead. Another warned them to beware of the Flatterer. The third told them not to sleep on Enchanted Ground, and the fourth wished them success and safety for their journey ahead.

I then woke from my dream.

An Encounter with Ignorance

As I slept and dreamed again, I saw Christian and Hopeful descending from the mountains on the highway heading toward the Celestial City. A little below these mountains, on the left side of the path, lay the country of Conceit. There was a little crooked path coming from this country that met up with the Way, and it was here that the two pilgrims met a very lively young man named Ignorance.

Christian approached the man and asked, "Where are you from, and where are you going?"

"Sir, I was born in the country of Conceit," he said, pointing back to the crooked path, "and I'm going to the Celestial City."

Christian appeared confused as he glanced back at the crooked path and then again at Ignorance. "But how do you expect to be admitted at the gate? Don't you think you might find it difficult to gain entrance there?"

Ignorance just shrugged. "I can't imagine why. I plan to enter just the same as other good people do."

"But what qualifications do you have to show at that gate so that it will be opened for you?"

"I know God's will and have lived a good life," Ignorance said with an air of confidence. "I've repaid all my debts, and I pray, fast, tithe, and give to charity. And what's more, I've left my own country to go there."

"But you did not enter at the Wicket Gate, which is at the beginning of the Way. You came in by means of that crooked path," Christian said, pointing back to the path. "I'm afraid that whatever you may think of yourself, when the day of final reckoning comes, you will be guilty of being a thief and a robber and will not gain entrance into the city."

"Gentlemen," said Ignorance with a slight smirk, "we're strangers, and I don't know you, so why don't you be content to follow your own religion and let me follow mine in hopes that all will be well. And as for the Wicket Gate that you mentioned, everyone around here knows that it's quite a distance away. I doubt anyone even knows how to get there, but it doesn't matter anyway. After all, we have, as you can see, a fine, pleasant green path that leads from our country right down to the Way."

When Christian saw that the man was wise in his own eyes, he whispered to Hopeful, "There's more hope for a fool than him. When a fool walks along the Way, his wisdom fails him, and he demonstrates to all that he is a fool." [154]

Christian was disappointed that he was not able to get through to Ignorance. "Should we talk with him more or walk on ahead and leave him to think about all he has heard? Perhaps we could stop again later to see if, by then, we can help him?"

Hopeful thought about it for a moment and said, "Yes, let's leave Ignorance alone to think about all that has been said in hopes that he will not later refuse to accept good counsel. Otherwise, he will remain ignorant of the truth. God has said that although he made them, he will not save them just because they do not understand."

Hopeful continued, "I don't think it's wise to tell him everything at once. If you agree, let's move ahead and plan to

---

[154] Prov. 26:12, Ecc. 10:3

talk with him again later when he's better prepared to receive it."

Christian and Hopeful went on their way while Ignorance followed behind them. After creating some distance between them, they entered a very dark path where they saw a man who had been bound with seven strong cords by seven devils. The devils were carrying the man back to the door the pilgrims had seen on the side of the hill when they were with the shepherds.[155]

Both Christian and Hopeful were terrified as they watched the devils lead the man away. Christian looked to see if he knew the man, thinking it might be Turn-away, who lived in the town of Apostasy.

But he could not clearly see his face, because the man hung his head like a thief who had been caught. Hopeful watched as he was taken away and noticed a paper with this inscription: "Reckless and uncontrolled professor and damnable apostate."

---

[155] Matt. 12:45, Prov. 5:22

The Assault on Little Faith

While Christian and Hopeful were reflecting on the tragic end of Turn-away, Christian said, "This reminds me of another story that I heard about something that happened to a good man named Little Faith. He lived in this region over in the town of Sincere."

Christian then began to relay the story as he had been told. "There's an entrance to the Way called Dead Man's Lane that comes down from Broadway Gate. It's a dangerous path because of the many murders committed there. Like us, Little Faith was going on a pilgrimage and just happened to sit down in that intersection and fell asleep. About that time, three strong villains named Faint Heart, Mistrust, and Guilt, who were brothers, came down the lane from Broadway Gate. When they spotted Little Faith sleeping beside the Way, they sprinted toward him.

"Little Faith was just waking up and getting ready to continue his journey when the three brutes approached him, threatening his life and ordering him to his feet. Little Faith turned white as a sheet and did not have the strength to fight nor flee.

"Faint Heart demanded, 'Hand over your money!'

"But Little Faith was slow to respond because he was reluctant to lose his money. Mistrust, seeing an opportunity, rushed in, thrust his hand into one of Little Faith's pockets, and pulled out a bag of silver.

"No sooner had Little Faith cried out, 'Thieves, thieves!' than Guilt moved in and struck Little Faith on the head with a big club, knocking him to the ground. The thieves just stood around watching him bleed to death until they heard others on the road. Fearing that it might be Great Grace, who lives in the town of Good Confidence, they quickly turned and ran away, leaving their victim to fend for himself."

Christian paused for a moment and then concluded his story. "After a while, Little Faith came to and managed to get to his feet. He staggered along on his pilgrimage the best he could."

Saddened by the story, Hopeful asked, "But did the thieves steal everything from him?"

"No," Christian said, shaking his head. "They never checked the pocket where he kept his jewels, so he was able to keep those. But as it was told to me, the thieves got most of his spending money, which left him overcome with grief. As I said, they did not get his jewels, but the little bit of money he did have left was not nearly enough to last him the rest of his journey.

"Unless I was misinformed, he was forced to beg while traveling just to stay alive for he would not sell his jewels. He traveled like this the rest of the way, scratching out a living but mostly on an empty stomach."[156]

"Isn't it remarkable that the thieves did not steal his certificate that would allow him entrance into the Celestial Gate?" Hopeful asked curiously.

"Yes, it is remarkable, but they did not get it," replied Christian. "It was not due to any cunning on the part of Little Faith though. He was caught off guard when they attacked him and did not have the power or skill to hide anything. This is a

---

[156] 1 Pet. 4:18

credit more to good providence rather than any effort on his part that they missed such a valuable item."[157]

Hopeful nodded in agreement. "Nevertheless, he must have been comforted by the fact that they did not steal his jewels."

"The jewels might have been a great comfort to him had he appreciated them as he should have. But as it was explained to me, he spoke little about the jewels for most of his journey because he was so distraught over losing his money. In fact, he mostly forgot about them, but occasionally, when he did think about them, he was quickly overwhelmed by the thought of the loss of his spending money."

"What a sad story about this poor man!" Hopeful said, shaking his head. "I'm sure his situation was a continual source of grief to him."

"Grief? Oh yes, he was deeply distressed!" said Christian. "I'm sure either one of us would be feeling the same had we been robbed and assaulted like he was in such a terrible place. It's a wonder that he did not die full of grief, poor soul! I was told that he was depressed and bitterly complained over his loss for the rest of his journey. He would tell everyone he encountered on the Way how he was robbed, who robbed and assaulted him, and that he barely escaped with his life."

"It's surprising that he did not try to sell or pawn some of the jewels to make his journey a little more comfortable," said Hopeful.

Christian's eyebrows raised in surprise as he was astounded by Hopeful's comment. "You're talking like a child! What reason would he ever have to sell his jewels, and who would he pawn them to? In the country where he was robbed, his jewels are not even considered valuable nor did he want relief from the citizens that lived there. Besides, he knew that if his jewels were missing at the gate of the Celestial City, he would

---

157 2 Tim. 1:12–14; 2 Pet. 2:9

never receive his inheritance there. That would have been worse to him than the wicked schemes of ten thousand thieves."

"Why are you being so sharp with me, Christian?" Hopeful said then countered, "Esau sold his birthright for a pot of stew, and that birthright was his greatest jewel! So if he sold such a valuable treasure, why could Little Faith not do the same?"[158]

Christian could not believe what he was hearing. "You're right. Esau did sell his birthright and so have many others, but in doing so, they have excluded themselves from receiving the ultimate blessing, just as that coward Esau did. Surely you must see the difference between the spiritual condition of Esau and that of Little Faith. Esau despised his birthright, but Little Faith valued his jewels. Esau's god was his stomach, but Little Faith's was not. Esau was driven by his worldly passions, but this was not true with Little Faith. Besides, Esau could see no further than to the fulfilling of his lusts when he said, 'For I am at the point of death so what good will a birthright do me?'[159]

"But Little Faith, though he was given just a little faith, was kept from such extremes. This same faith caused him to value his jewels rather than sell them as Esau did his birthright.

"You will not read anywhere of the faith of Esau, not even a little. Therefore, it's not surprising in the case of Esau that he was controlled by his desires. For where there is no faith to resist, one will sell his birthright, his soul, and everything that he has, even to the devil in Hell. This man can be compared to a wild donkey in heat that cannot be turned away.[160] When their minds are set upon their lusts, they will have them, whatever the cost.

---

[158] Heb. 12:16
[159] Gen. 25:32
[160] Jer. 2:24

"No, Little Faith was a true pilgrim. His mind was focused on the things of God, and his livelihood was based on spiritual matters from Heaven. Therefore, what reason would someone of his character have to sell his jewels? If there had been anyone interested in buying them, it would only serve to fill his mind with empty things. Will a man give a penny to eat hay when he's hungry? Or can you persuade a turtledove to feast on the decaying flesh of dead animals like a crow? Those without faith will pawn, mortgage, or sell what they have—and even themselves outright to fulfill their sexual desires. But those that have a saving faith, even just a little of it, cannot do so. Hopeful, this is where you are mistaken."

Hopeful was becoming a little annoyed with Christian's harsh tone. "I can acknowledge my error, but I must admit that your severe response has almost made me angry."

"Do not take offense," Christian said, placing a hand on Hopeful's shoulder. "I only did so to compare your understanding of the matter to that of a baby bird that eagerly runs back and forth, not knowing where they're going, with their shells still upon their heads. But let's leave this matter behind us and consider it under debate, and all will be well between you and me."

Hopeful nodded in agreement, but then countered once again, "But, Christian, I believe with all my heart that those who attacked Little Faith were nothing but cowards. Why else would they have run so quickly when they heard someone approaching on the road? And why wasn't Little Faith more courageous? In my opinion, he might have been able to stand his ground for a while before being overpowered."

"Most will agree with you that these assailants are cowards, but few have found this to be the case when they are the ones being assaulted," replied Christian. "As for Little Faith having a courageous heart, he had no such thing. And I'm confident, my brother, that had the same thing happened to you, you would have surrendered quickly too. In all fairness, it's easy to be courageous while these men are far off, but you might have second thoughts if they suddenly appeared to challenge you now as they did him.

"Also, let's not forget that these men are hired thieves who serve under the king of the bottomless pit, and if needed, he will come to their aid, roaring like a lion.[161]

"I myself experienced a conflict much like Little Faith's and found it terrifying. These three villains attacked me, and I began to resist them as a Christian should; they quickly called for help, and their master came right away. As the saying goes, 'I would have given my life for a penny.' However, God had other plans and I was clothed in battle-tested armor, but even though I was well equipped, I found it difficult to prove myself spiritually mature. No one can understand what it's like to experience such combat until they have been in the thick of the battle themselves."

Hopeful considered what Christian had said then responded confidently, "Well, there's no doubt that those thieves ran away when they thought Great Grace was on the road."

"That's true!" Christian agreed. "They and their master have often fled when they feared Great Grace was close. But why should we be surprised since he's the King's champion? I trust you will allow some distinction between Little Faith and the King's champion. Not all the King's subjects are his champions nor can they accomplish such feats of war as he when attacked. Is it reasonable to expect that a little child could handle Goliath as David did or that a small bird should have the strength of an ox? Some pilgrims are strong, while others are weak; some have great faith, while some have little. This man Little Faith was one of the weaker types, and therefore he suffered exhaustion and humiliation."

---

[161] 1 Pet. 5:8

Hopeful sighed. "I still wish Great Grace had arrived to take care of those thieves."

"If he had, he might have had his hands full," said Christian. "There's no doubt that Great Grace is a highly skilled warrior with excellent weapons, and with a sharp sword, he can do very well against such opponents. But if Faint Heart, Mistrust, or Guilt can get close enough to penetrate his armor. he will fall hard. As you know, when a man is down, what else can he do?

"Whoever looks closely at the face of Great Grace will see scars and cuts that clearly prove what I'm saying. I heard it reported that he even despaired for his life once in battle. Is it not true that these rogues and their accomplices were able to make David groan, mourn, and roar in suffering? And they did the same to Heman[162] and Hezekiah too! Even though they were champions in their days, they were forced to take a stand when assaulted by these thieves and still took quite a beating. On one occasion, Peter, who some say is the prince of the apostles, was so roughed up by them that he became afraid of a servant girl.

"Besides, their evil king is always listening for their call, and if at any time they are losing in battle, he will, whenever possible, come to their aid. For this reason, it has been said of him, 'No sword, spear, dart, or javelin that strikes him will succeed. He regards iron as straw and bronze as rotten wood. Arrows will not make him flee. Sling-stones are turned by him into rubble. Darts are considered straw. He laughs at the rattling of spears.' What can a man do in this situation?

"No doubt if this man had full access to Job's horse and the skill and courage to ride him, he might do extraordinary things for his king. For it's said of this horse that his neck is clothed with thunder and it's not afraid like a grasshopper. He strikes

---

[162] Ps. 88

179

terror with the snorting of his nostrils. He paws in the valley and rejoices in his strength and then charges in to meet armed men. He laughs at fear, afraid of nothing, and will never shy away from the sword. The quiver rattles against his side as do the flashing spear and shield. As he runs, he eats up the ground with fierceness and rage and cannot stand still when the trumpet sounds. Rather at the blast of the trumpets he snorts, 'Aha!' and catches the scent of a distant battle and the thundering of the captains with their battle cry."[163]

"But Hopeful, we are mere foot soldiers and should never desire to meet an enemy in battle nor boast that we could do better when hearing of others who have been defeated. Nor should we entertain thoughts that our own spiritual maturity is braver than it is, because those that think this way often suffer the worst when tried. Take Peter, for example, whom I mentioned earlier. He would parade his bravery; indeed he would. Because of his pride, he considered himself ready to stand and defend his Master above all other men. But tell me, who was more defeated and scared than he when these villains were on the attack?

"So when we hear of such attacks taking place on the King's highway, we should respond in two ways:

"First, let's be well equipped with our weapons, especially a shield. For it was the lack of a shield that made it impossible for the brave warrior who attacked Leviathan to make him surrender. It's true that if our shield is missing, he does not fear us at all. That is why a skilled warrior like Paul said, 'Above all take the shield of faith with which you will be able to extinguish all the flaming arrows of the evil one.'[164]

"Secondly, it's also good to request the convoy of the King and that He will go with us Himself. This prospect made David

---

[163] Job 39:19–25
[164] Eph. 6:16

rejoice when he passed through the Valley of the Shadow of Death, and Moses said he would prefer dying where he stood rather than to go one more step without his God."[165]

Christian clasped his hands together. "Oh, Hopeful! If our King will just go along with us, why should we be afraid of ten thousand who would plot against us?[166] But without our King, the proud will only find refuge hiding under the dead.[167]

"As for myself, I've been in the thick of battle before, and as you can see, I'm still alive only because of His goodness and grace, not because of great spiritual maturity on my part. I would be glad to never experience any more such attacks, but I fear we have not passed beyond all danger. However, since the lion and the bear have not yet devoured me, I hope God will also deliver us from the next uncircumcised Philistine."

Then sang Christian,

Poor Little Faith has been among the thieves!
Was robbed! Remember this, whosoever believes,
And get more faith, shall then a victor be
Over ten thousand, otherwise not even three.

---

165 Ex. 33:15
166 Ps. 3:5–8, 27:1–3
167 Isa. 10:4

Chapter Eleven

The Ensnarement of Flatterer

Christian and Hopeful continued walking along the Way, with Ignorance still trailing behind them. Before long, they came upon another path that joined the Way. The new path appeared to go in the same direction as the path they were on, so they stood there wondering which path to take.

As they were thinking, a dark man wearing a very light-colored robe approached and asked, "Why are you standing here?"

"We're going to the Celestial City," they replied, "but we're not sure which of these paths to take."

"Come with me, then," the man said with authority, motioning to the new path. "I'm also going to the Celestial City."

Christian and Hopeful followed their guide along the new path that had joined the Way, but over time, the path gradually veered away from the Celestial City, taking them in the opposite direction. They continued to follow him because they were not yet aware of his deception, but before they knew what was happening, he led them straight into a net where they became completely entangled, not knowing what to do.

Suddenly, the white robe fell off the dark man's back, and

the captives began to realize what had happened. Therefore, they laid around crying for some time because they could not escape the net.

Christian turned to Hopeful and said, "Now I see my error. Didn't the shepherds warn us to beware of Flatterer? Today we have discovered the truth in the sayings of the wise, 'Those who flatter their neighbors are spreading nets for their feet.'"[168]

Hopeful nodded in agreement while eagerly trying to free himself. "They also gave us written directions for the Way to make sure we arrived safely, but we have forgotten to read it and have not kept ourselves out of the paths of the destroyer. In this, David was much wiser than us when he said, 'Though people have tried to bribe me, I have kept myself from the ways of the violent through what your lips have commanded."[169]

They laid there, entangled in the net, groaning and complaining until they saw an angel coming toward them with a whip made of small cords in his hand.

When he came close to the place where they were, he asked, "Where are you from, and what are you doing here?"

With quivering voices, they replied, "We are poor pilgrims going to the Celestial City, but we were led astray by a dark man clothed in white who told us to follow him because he was going there too."

Then the angel replied, "It's Flatterer, a false apostle, who has transformed himself into an angel of light."[170]

He tore open the net and freed its captives, saying, "Follow me, and I will put you on the right way again."

---

[168] Prov. 29:5
[169] Ps. 17:4
[170] Dan. 11:32, 2 Cor. 11:13–14

He led them back to the straight Way, which they had left to follow Flatterer, and asked them, "Where did you sleep last night?"

"With the shepherds on the Delectable Mountains," they replied, pointing in the direction of the mountains.

The angel looked surprised and asked, "Did the shepherds not provide you written directions for the Way?"

"Yes," they confessed sheepishly.

"When you were trying to decide which way to go, did you not refer to the map for guidance?" he asked.

"No," they replied, feeling somewhat foolish.

"Well, why not?" he asked.

Christian and Hopeful shared an embarrassing glance and said, "We forgot."

"Did the shepherds not also tell you to beware of Flatterer?" he asked.

"Yes, but we could not imagine that this gentleman who spoke so well and was dressed so nice was he," they replied.[171]

Then, in my dream, I saw that he ordered them to lie down, and once they did, he whipped them severely to teach them the good way where they should walk.[172] While he was chastising them, he said, "Those whom I love I rebuke and discipline. So be earnest and repent."[173]

Afterward, he sent them on their way, telling them to pay better attention to the shepherds' directions. They thanked him for all his kindness and went along the right way, softly singing,

---

[171] Rom. 16:17–18
[172] Deut. 25:2, 2 Chron. 6:27
[173] Rev. 3:19

Come here, you that walk along the Way,
See what happens to pilgrims who go astray.
They get caught in an entangling net,
Because the good counsel they lightly did forget:
It's true they were rescued, but as you see,
They're scourged as well; let this your caution be.

The Laughter of Atheist

Now, after a while, they noticed someone in the distance walking toward them quietly and all alone on the highway.

Christian turned to Hopeful. "Here comes a man walking in the opposite direction of Zion coming up to meet us."

"I see him," said Hopeful suspiciously. "Let's be more cautious this time as he might also turn out to be a Flatterer."

The man drew closer and closer until at last he came up to them. His name was Atheist, and he asked the pilgrims where they were going.

"We're going to Mount Zion," said Christian while cautiously eyeing the man.

Atheist burst into a howling laughter.

Christian glanced at Hopeful, shrugging his shoulders, and then back at the man. "Why are you laughing?"

"I cannot help but laugh on account of your ignorance!" he said, doubled over and chuckling. "You've committed yourself to a very tiring journey and will likely have nothing to show for it except pain."

Christian's face grew concerned. "Why do you say that? Do you think we will not be received?"

"Received!" boomed Atheist, still laughing. "There's no such place in all the world that you are dreaming about."

Christian looked confused. "But there is in the world to come."

Atheist shook his head as he began to gain his composure. "When I was at home in my own country, I also heard about this place you're talking about," he said, "so I went out to investigate it myself and have spent over 20 years looking for this city. But from the day that I first left home until now, I've found no such place."[174]

Christian said confidently, "Well, we've both heard and definitely believe that there is such a place to be found."

Atheist looked Christian and Hopeful up and down, smirked, and said, "When I was at home, I also heard and believed just as you do now and came all this way looking, but I found nothing. You would think that if such a place existed, I would have found it by now as I've traveled much farther than you. Now I'm going back home, where I hope to refresh myself with the things that I previously tossed away when I went searching for the hope of something that cannot be found."

Christian glanced over at Hopeful with a serious look and said, "Do you think it's true what this man is telling us?"

"Be very careful!" Hopeful said sternly. "This man is definitely one of the Flatterers. Remember what it already cost us for listening to a smooth-talker such as Atheist. What a thing to say, that there is no Celestial City! Did we not see with our own eyes the very gate of the city from the top of the Delectable Mountains? Furthermore, are we not now to walk by faith?[175] Let us continue on our way or the man with the whip will catch up with us again!"

Hopeful seemed disappointed in Christian. "You should have taught me this lesson that I'm now teaching you when I

---

[174] Ecc. 10:15, Jer. 17:15
[175] 2 Cor. 5:7

say, 'If you stop listening to instruction, my son, you will stray from the words of knowledge.'[176] I will tell you, my brother, that we should stop listening to Atheist and rather believe in the saving of the soul."

Christian smiled proudly. "My brother, I confess that I did not ask you the question because I personally doubted the truth. Rather, my intention was to test you and bring forth a response that indicated the real commitment of your heart." He gestured toward Atheist. "As for this man, I know that he's blinded by the god of this world. Let's continue on knowing that we believe in the truth and there can be no lie in the truth."[177]

"Now I do rejoice in the hope of the glory of God!" Hopeful said.

They turned away from Atheist while he, still laughing, went on his way back home.

---

[176] Prov. 19:27
[177] 1 John 2:21

Crossing the Enchanted Ground

Then I saw in my dream that Christian and Hopeful continued traveling until they came to a certain region where the air naturally tended to make unsuspecting travelers drowsy. It was here that Hopeful became lethargic and sleepy. He slowed his pace, yawned, and suggested to Christian, "I'm becoming so drowsy that I can barely hold my eyes open. Let's lie down here and take a nap."

"Absolutely not!" Christian said adamantly. "If we fall asleep here, we might never wake up again."

Not understanding, Hopeful rubbed his eyes. "Why do you say that? Sleep is sweet to the working man. If we take a nap, we will be refreshed for the journey ahead."

"Don't you remember what one of the shepherds told us?" Christian said as he shook Hopeful's shoulder, trying to wake him. "He told us to beware of the Enchanted Ground, which means that we should be careful not to sleep there. So let's not fall asleep like others. Let's stay awake and be alert."[178]

"I confess that I've made a mistake," Hopeful said, stretching. "If I'd been here alone and fallen asleep, I likely would have died. How true is the wise saying, 'Two are better than one.'[179] I'm truly blessed because of your companionship

---

[178] 1 Thess. 5:6
[179] Ecc. 4:9

and you should be rewarded well for your efforts.'"

"Now then," Christian said, slapping Hopeful on the back, "let's talk about something worthwhile to prevent us from becoming any sleepier."

"I wholeheartedly agree!" said Hopeful.

"Then where should we start?"

"Well, how about where God began with us," Hopeful suggested. "Why don't you go first?"

"That'll be fine!" Christian agreed. "But first let me sing you this song:

"When saints grow sleepy, let them come close,
And hear how these two pilgrims talk together,
Yes, let them learn of them in any wise way,
So as to keep open their drowsy, slumbering eyes.
Saints' fellowship, if it be managed well,
Keeps them awake, and that in spite of Hell."

Then Christian began their discussion with a question. "Hopeful, I'm curious. When did you first begin to think about going on this pilgrimage?"

Hopeful looked puzzled. "Do you mean when did I first become concerned about the condition of my soul?"

Christian nodded. "Yes, that's exactly what I mean."

"Well, I lived for a long time fulfilling my desires with the things marketed and sold at Vanity Fair," he said. "These are things, which, as I now believe, had I continued in them still, would have led to my destruction and eternal damnation."

"Things like what?" Christian asked curiously.

"Why, all the treasures and riches of the world!" Hopeful said with his hands in the air. "I took great pleasure in extravagant living, wild parties, drinking, swearing, lying, immorality, Sabbath breaking, and much more, all of which were destroying my soul. But when I began to hear about spiritual truth from listening to both you and our dear friend Faithful, who was put to death for his faith and godly living in Vanity Fair, I discovered that my ungodly lifestyle would eventually lead to my death.[180] I also learned that God's wrath will come on those who are disobedient."

"With this new understanding, did you immediately fall under the power of this conviction?" asked Christian.

"No," admitted Hopeful, shaking his head. "At that time, I was not ready to understand the evils of sin or the damnation that results from obeying it. Instead, it was the exact opposite. When God's truth first began to convict me, I tried to block it from my mind and turn a blind eye to what it was revealing in my life."

"But why did you continue to resist the first workings of God's blessed Spirit on you?"

"For a variety of reasons," Hopeful said. "First of all, I did not understand that this conviction was the work of God in me and that He begins the conversation with a sinner by making them aware of their sin. Secondly, I enjoyed my sin and was hesitant to leave it. Thirdly, I didn't know how to part ways with my old friends whose company and lifestyle I continued to enjoy. And finally, when I felt the weight of this conviction over my sin, it terrified me so that I could not bear to think about the guilt it left behind on my heart."

Christian considered the answer and replied, "So what you're saying is that occasionally you were able to resist your conviction?"

"Yes, that's true," Hopeful said, nodding. "But then it would return to my thoughts again, and I would be as bad— no, even worse—than I was before!"

---

[180] Rom. 6:23

"Why?" Christian said, probing. "What was it that made you think about your sins again?"

"Many things, for example, if I met a man around town who was doing what was right and good, if I heard the Bible read or mentioned, if I was sick, if I heard that one of my neighbors was sick, if I heard the bell toll for someone who had died, if I thought of dying myself, or if I heard that someone had died unexpectedly." Hopeful stopped and looked at Christian. "But especially when I considered that I would eventually die and stand in judgment before God."

"When you were confronted with any of these situations, were you able to easily dismiss the guilt you were feeling over your sin?" asked Christian.

"No, I could not. When I thought of returning to sin, my conscience was completely overcome with guilt—even though my mind was content to remain in sin. I was tormented on both sides!"

"Then what did you decide to do?"

"I decided it was time to try to become a better person or else I would be damned for sure."

"Were you successful in becoming a better person?"

"Yes," said Hopeful confidently, "I fled from my sins and from sinful company. I also devoted myself to religious activities, such as praying, reading, weeping over my sin, being honest with all my neighbors, and much more. I became involved in too many religious activities to mention!"

"With all this religious activity, did you now feel that your life was better off than before?"

"Yes…well, for a while anyway." Hopeful shrugged. "But even though I had made these efforts to become a better person, all of my troubles eventually returned and overwhelmed me again."

"How could this possibly have happened since you made all

this effort to change your ways and improve your life?" Christian said with a wink, already knowing the correct answer.

Hopeful let out a slight smile, sighed, and said, "There were several reasons why trying to be better by my own efforts failed, especially when you consider sayings such as 'All our righteous acts are like filthy rags,'[181] 'By the works of the law no one will be justified,'[182] 'When you have done everything you were told to do, you should say we are unworthy servants,'[183] and many more sayings just like this.

"It was then I began to understand that if all of my efforts to reform my life were just filthy rags; if trying to do what is right will not justify me; and, if after I've done all these things, I'm still unworthy, then it's foolish to think that I will ever be able to obtain Heaven by my own efforts."

He continued, "Think about it this way: If a man should run up a hundred dollars in debt at a local store and then pays cash for everything else that he buys, his original debt still remains unsettled. In this case, the store owner would be in his rights to sue the man and throw him into prison until he can pay the debt."

Christian interrupted Hopeful. "Yes, I understand what you're saying, but how does this apply to you?"

Hopeful held up his hand. "Well, I realized that all my sins have run up quite the debt in God's ledger book, and all my efforts to create a better life will never be able to pay off what I owe. So what good, then, were all these reforms I put in place? This left me wondering how I'll ever be free from the danger of damnation on account of my past sins."

Christian thought about it for a moment then said, "Yes,

---

[181] Is. 64:6
[182] Gal. 2:16
[183] Luke 17:10

that's a very good application, but please go on."

"Well, there was another thing that started to concern me when I began to make efforts to become a better person. When I looked closer at the best of my performance, I still saw sin, *new sin*, mixing in there right with it. So I was forced to conclude that despite feeling good about myself and my new efforts to improve my life, I've committed enough sin in one day to send me to Hell even if I had never sinned before."

Christian nodded while motioning for him to continue, saying, "And what did you do then, Hopeful?"

"What did I do?" Hopeful said, raising his voice. "I had no idea what to do until I shared all my concerns with my friend Faithful. He told me that the only way to be right with God is to attain perfect righteousness from a man who had never sinned. If not, no amount of my own righteousness nor all the righteousness in the world could save me."

"And did you think he was telling you the truth?" asked Christian.

"Honestly, had he told me this when I was happy and satisfied with my life, I would have called him a fool for telling me such things. But now, after having seen my own corruption and the sin attached to even my best efforts, I was compelled to agree with him."

"When Faithful first suggested it to you, did you think there was such a man that existed who could honestly be described as having never committed a sin?"

"I must confess that at first his words sounded strange, but after talking with Faithful a little more and spending time with him, I became fully convinced that he was right."

"And did you ask him who this man was and to explain how you go about being justified by Him?"

Hopeful nodded. "Yes, and he told me that this man was the

Lord Jesus, who lives at the right hand of the Most High.[184] He then explained that to be justified by Him, I must trust in what Jesus accomplished when He suffered while hanging on the cross.[185] I asked him how one man's righteousness could successfully justify another man before God, and he told me that Jesus *was* the mighty God and that what He did by dying on the cross was not for Himself but for me. The righteousness of His atoning work and its worthiness would be credited to me if I believed on Him."

"And did you believe then?"

Hopeful shook his head. "I offered objections as to why I should not believe, because I thought Jesus was not willing to save me."

"And what did Faithful tell you then?"

"He urged me to go to Jesus to find out for myself," said Hopeful. "I said I thought that would be presumptuous on my part, but Faithful said it wasn't since I was invited to do so.[186] Then he gave me a book that contained the teachings of Jesus to encourage me to freely come to Him, saying that every word in the book is more true than anything found in this world.[187]

"So I asked Faithful what I must do when I came to Christ, and he told me that I must fall on my knees and plead with all my heart and soul for the Father to reveal Him to me.[188] I then asked him how I should go about approaching Him. He told me to go find Christ sitting on the mercy seat, where He sits all year long providing mercy and forgiveness to all that come to Him.[189]

---

[184] Heb. 10:12–21
[185] Rom. 4:5, Col. 1:14, 1 Pet. 1:19
[186] Matt. 11:28
[187] Matt. 24:35
[188] Ps. 95:6, Dan. 6:10, Jer. 29:12–13
[189] Ex. 25:22, Lev. 16:2, Num. 7:89, Heb. 4:16

"I told him that I didn't know what to say when I came. He guided me to say something like, 'God have mercy on a sinner like me and enable me to know and believe in Jesus Christ. For I understand that if the righteousness of Christ was not available or if I didn't have faith in that righteousness, then I would be utterly rejected from your presence. Lord, I've heard that you're a merciful God and have ordained that your Son, Jesus Christ, should be the Savior of the world. Additionally, I've heard that you're willing to extend His salvation to even a poor sinner like me—and I'm without a doubt a poor sinner. Therefore, Lord, take this opportunity to magnify Your grace in the salvation of my soul through your Son Jesus Christ. Amen.'"

"And did you do exactly as you were instructed?" asked Christian.

Hopeful nodded. "Yes, over, and over, and over again."

"And did the Father reveal His Son to you?"

"Not on the first, the second, the third, the fourth, the fifth, or even the sixth time," said Hopeful, shaking his head.

"Then what did you do?"

"What did I do?" Hopeful said thoughtfully. "Well, I didn't know what to do then."

"Did you ever consider just giving up on praying?"

"Yes, at least a hundred times, maybe more!"

"Why did you not give up?"

"I believed what Faithful told me was true, that without the righteousness of Christ, all the world could not save me. I thought that if I stopped praying and I died in that moment, I would have stopped praying right at the throne of grace. And then I began to think that even if His saving grace should linger, I should wait for it because it will certainly come and without delay.[190] So I continued praying until the Father showed me His Son."

"And how was He eventually revealed to you?" Christian asked.

"I did not see Him with physical eyes but rather with eyes of understanding."[191] Then Hopeful began to relay the story. "One day I was very sad. In fact, I think I was more depressed than at any other time in my life, and it was because of fresh insight into how great and repulsive my sins were. As I was anticipating nothing but Hell and eternal damnation of my soul, suddenly I thought I saw the Lord Jesus looking down from Heaven on me, saying, 'Believe on the Lord Jesus Christ and you will be saved.'[192]

"But I replied, 'Lord, I'm a very great sinner,' and He answered, 'My grace is enough for you.'[193]

"Then I said, 'But, Lord, what exactly is believing?' Immediately, I understood the saying, 'Whoever comes to me will never go hungry, and whoever believes in me will never be thirsty.'[194] I also understood that believing and coming were the same thing. The one who's heart honestly desires the salvation of Christ is the one who truly believes in Christ.

"As tears filled my eyes, I asked further, 'But, Lord, may such a great sinner as I am actually be accepted and saved by you?'

"And I heard Him say, 'Whoever comes to me I will never cast away.'[195]

"Then I responded, 'But, Lord, what is the appropriate way

---

[190] Hab. 2:3
[191] Eph. 1:18–19
[192] Acts 16:31
[193] 2 Cor. 12:9
[194] John 6:35
[195] John 6:37

for me to come so that my faith is properly placed on you?'

"Then He said, 'Jesus Christ came into the world to save sinners.[196] He is the end of the law for righteousness to all who believe.[197] He died for our sins and rose again for our justification.[198] He loved us and washed us from our sins in His own blood.[199] He is the mediator between God and us.[200] He lives to make intercession for us.'[201]

"It was from all of this that I understood I must look for righteousness in the person of Jesus Christ and for satisfaction for my sins by His blood. In obedience, Christ submitted to the penalty of His Father's law for those who will accept it for their salvation with thankfulness. As a result, my heart was full of joy, my eyes flooded with tears, and my affections overflowed with love for the name, people, and ways of Jesus Christ."

"This was truly a revelation of Christ to your soul!" Christian exclaimed, clasping his hands together. "But tell me more specifically what change this had on your spirit and your view of the world."

Hopeful thought about it for a minute and said, "It helped me see that this entire world, despite all its allure and attraction, is in a state of condemnation and that a righteous God can also make sinners righteous before Him. Also, I was greatly ashamed for the sin of my past lifestyle while amazed that I could be so ignorant to have never thought about the beauty of Christ before.

"Finally, it made me love the pursuit of holiness and long to

---

[196] 1 Tim. 1:15
[197] Rom. 10:4
[198] Rom. 4:25
[199] Rev. 1:5
[200] 1 Tim 2:5
[201] Heb. 7:25

do something for the honor and glory of the name of the Lord Jesus. Yes, I believed without a doubt that if I had a thousand gallons of blood in my body, I would willingly spill it all for the sake of the Lord Jesus!"

Ignorance Follows His Heart

As they continued walking, Hopeful looked back and saw Ignorance, whom they had left earlier, following them.

"Look how far that young man has fallen behind," Hopeful said, pointing back at Ignorance.

"Oh yes, I see him," said Christian, looking out into the distance, "but he doesn't care much for our company."

"I know," said Hopeful, slowing his pace. "But it wouldn't have hurt him had he decided to walk with us to this point."

Christian smiled. "That's true, but I'm certain he thinks otherwise."

"I'm sure he does," said Hopeful, smiling back. "However, let's wait for him."

As they slowed down, Christian called out to Ignorance, "Hurry up, man! Why are you lagging so far behind?"

Ignorance glanced up at the two pilgrims in front of him and replied bluntly, "I enjoy walking alone rather than in a group, that is, unless I *like* those in the group."

Christian glanced over at Hopeful with an eyebrow raised. "See, I told you that he doesn't care for our company." He then yelled back to Ignorance, "Catch up and we'll spend some time talking together in this peaceful place."

As soon as Ignorance caught up to them, Christian said,

"Tell us how you're doing and how your relationship is between God and your soul since we last spoke."

"I hope all is well," said Ignorance, shrugging his shoulders. "I always fill my mind with good thoughts that comfort me as I walk along the Way."

Christian was curious. "Please tell us more about these good thoughts."

"Why, I think about God and Heaven," he replied confidently.

Christian furrowed his forehead and countered, "So do the demons and every soul that is destined for Hell."

Ignorance smiled at Christian's response. "Yes, but I think about them and also desire them."

"So do many others that will likely never go to Heaven. It's like the proverb goes, 'The slacker craves but has nothing.'"[202]

"Perhaps," he replied. "But I think about them and have left everything for them."

"I doubt that very much," said Christian, "because to leave everything is much more difficult than most people understand. What evidence has convinced you that you've left everything for God and Heaven?"

Ignorance placed his hand on his chest. "My heart tells me so."

"The wise man said that those who trust in their own hearts are fools," Christian replied.[203]

Ignorance waved him off. "That saying is referring to an evil heart, but mine is a good one."

"But how can you prove that your heart is as good as you say it is?"

---

[202] Prov. 13:4
[203] Prov. 28:26

"Because it comforts me regarding my hope of going to Heaven."

"That may be so, but the heart can be deceitful," Christian said. "You see, our hearts may provide us comfort when we hope for something even though we have no reason to expect that hope to be fulfilled."

Ignorance held up his hand as if to object. "Yes, but my heart and life are in agreement with each other, so there's reason for my hope."

"Who told you that your heart and life are in agreement?" Christian asked.

Ignorance hesitated for a moment and then answered, "Well, my heart tells me so."

"My dear man, if your heart told you that you're a thief, would you believe it?" asked Christian in a fatherly tone. "Your heart may tell you one thing, but it's God's Word that must prove whether it's true or not."

Ignorance looked confused. "But doesn't a good heart produce good thoughts? And isn't a good life one that's in accordance with God's commands?"

"Yes, that's true," Christian admitted. "However, it's one thing to actually have those qualities and another thing to only think that you do."

"Then tell me," said Ignorance, "what do you consider to be good thoughts and a good life according to the commands of God?"

"There are many different types of good thoughts," Christian said, "some with regard to ourselves, some God, some Christ, and some other things."

Now Ignorance took his turn asking some questions. "All right, then, what are good thoughts with regard to ourselves?"

"It would be those thoughts that are in agreement with

God's Word."

"When do thoughts of ourselves agree with God's Word?"

"When we pass the same judgment on ourselves that God would pass on us, then we're in agreement with God's Word."

Seeing that Ignorance was confused, Christian continued, "Let me see if I can explain it better. The Word of God says of our natural condition, 'There's no one who is righteous, not even one.'[204] It also says, 'Every inclination of the thoughts of the human heart was only evil all the time,'[205] and again, 'Every inclination of the human heart is evil from childhood.'[206] Now, then, when we think about ourselves in this sense, our thoughts can only be good when they're in agreement with God's Word."

Ignorance crossed his arms. "I'll never believe that my heart is bad."

Christian shook his head in disappointment. "If that's true, then you've never had one good thought about yourself in your whole life."

Ignorance started to interrupt, but Christian cut him off. "Let me continue. As God's Word passes judgment on our hearts, so it also passes judgment on our actions. When the thoughts of our hearts and our actions agree with the truth found in God's Word, then both are good."

Ignorance was still confused. "Please explain what you mean."

"Absolutely," Christian said. "God's Word says that our ways are not good but rather crooked and perverse. It also says that by nature, we will turn from the good way and are predisposed to not even realize it. Now, when we consider our

---

[204] Rom. 3:10
[205] Gen. 6:5
[206] Gen. 8:21

actions in this way, with a sensitive and humble heart, then we will have good thoughts about our own ways. Our thoughts now agree with the judgment of God's Word."

Ignorance was quiet for a while as he contemplated this new information. "Then what exactly are good thoughts about God?" he said.

"Good thoughts about God are similar to what I said concerning ourselves. When our thoughts about God agree with what the Word says about Him, then they're good thoughts. In other words, to rightly think about God is to think about His character and attributes exactly as the Word has taught.

"However, I cannot speak about this in too much detail now except to say that when we speak of God concerning ourselves, we must understand that He knows us better than we know ourselves and can see sin in us even when we cannot. It's then that we have the right thoughts about God. When we understand that He knows our innermost thoughts and can always see into the depths of our hearts, and when we understand that all our righteousness stinks in his nostrils and that even with our best performance we still cannot stand before Him with any confidence, then we know our thoughts are good."

Ignorance snickered. "Do you think that I'm such a fool as to believe that God can see no further than I can? Do you also think that I would hope to come to God for acceptance of only my best performances?"

"Then tell me," Christian said, "what do you think concerning this matter?"

Ignorance crossed his arms. "Well, I'll come straight to the point. I think I must believe in Christ for justification."

"But how!" Christian blurted out. "How can you believe in Christ when you don't see any need for him? You don't see your original sin or your actual transgressions but rather have such a high opinion of yourself. In fact, your actions clearly qualify you as one who has never seen the necessity of Christ's personal righteousness to justify you before God. How then can you possibly say that you believe in Christ?"

"In spite of what you say, I believe well enough," said Ignorance, folding his arms.

Christian persisted, "But exactly what is it that you believe?"

"I believe that Christ died for sinners and that I will be justified before God from the curse of the law through His gracious acceptance of my obedience to His laws. In other words, Christ makes my religious duties acceptable to His Father by virtue of His merits, and so by this, I will be justified."

Christian paused for a moment to gather his thoughts. "Let me give an answer to this confession of your faith. First, you believe in an imaginary faith that's described nowhere in God's Word.

"Secondly, you believe in a false faith that removes the personal righteousness of Christ and applies it to you. In this false faith, you have Christ justifying your actions rather than you as a person. It's false to believe your actions will ever justify you.

"Therefore, this faith of yours is deceitful and will leave you under the wrath of God in the final day of judgment while convincing you that all is well. True justifying faith directs the soul, which is aware of its lost condition by the law, to flee for refuge into Christ's righteousness. This righteousness of Christ is not an act of grace by which He makes your obedience a justifying work acceptable to God. Rather, it's His personal obedience to the law in suffering for us, which this same law required of us. I can tell you that true faith accepts this righteousness as if it were a blanket that completely covers the soul. In this way, the soul is presented as spotless before God and is accepted and acquitted from condemnation."

"What are you saying?" said Ignorance. "Would you have us trust in what Christ has done on His own without us having to do anything? This explanation would surely give sin free reign and allow us to live as we want. What difference would it make then how we live if we can be justified from all our sin by Christ's personal righteousness and all we have to do is simply believe?"

Christian just shook his head. "Ignorance is your name, and it fits you well as you're an ignorant person. Even your answer demonstrates this to be true. You're ignorant of what justifying righteousness actually is and equally as ignorant as to how to secure saving faith from the heavy wrath of God through faith. Yes, you're also ignorant of the true effects of saving faith in this righteousness of Christ, which is to bow and surrender the heart to God in Christ to love His name, His Word, His ways, and His people and not as ignorantly as you imagine."

Hearing this discussion, Hopeful nudged Christian. "Ask him if God has ever opened his heart so that Christ might be revealed to him."

Ignorance heard Hopeful and said, "What's this now? Are you a man influenced by revelations? I'm convinced that what you and all the rest of your type say about God's grace is nothing more than fruit for distracted minds."

"Listen to me," Hopeful said directly. "God has hidden Christ from our natural understanding so that no one can be saved unless God the Father reveals Himself to them."

"That's your faith, but it's not mine," said Ignorance, pointing at Hopeful. "However, I have no doubt that my faith is as good as yours and without all of your fanciful thoughts in my head."

Hopeful softened his tone and said, "Please allow me to give you one more piece of advice. You shouldn't speak about sin so lightly. I will boldly affirm, even as my good friend has already done, that no man can know Jesus Christ except by the revelation of the Father. And what's more, I will also say that faith that takes hold of Christ, assuming it's a saving faith, must be molded into shape by the exceeding greatness of His mighty power.[207]

"Poor Ignorance. I believe that you're ignorant of the working of this faith. Wake up! Repent of your own wretchedness, and run to the Lord Jesus. Only by His righteousness, which is the righteousness of God, for He Himself is God, will you be delivered from condemnation."

"You go so fast I cannot keep up with you," Ignorance said, motioning for them to go on without him. "So do go on ahead as before, and I will follow from behind."

Then they said, "Very well, Ignorance, if you'll be so foolish as to ignore good counsel when provided repeatedly. And if you continue to refuse it, you will know the evil of doing so. Remember that in time, we should rise and not fear but rather listen to and accept good counsel because it saves. But if you should neglect it, you'll be the loser, Ignorance, I'll guarantee you."

---

[207] Matt. 11:27, 1 Cor. 12:3, Eph. 1:17-19

The Backsliding of Temporary

After leaving Ignorance behind, Christian turned to Hopeful and said, "Well, my good friend, it appears as though you and I must walk by ourselves again."

In my dream, they went on ahead quickly with Ignorance limping along behind them.

Christian glanced back at Ignorance and said, "I really do pity the poor man because his journey will come to a terrible end."

"It's very sad!" said Hopeful. "In our own town, there are so many people who are just like him—whole families, even whole streets, and some claiming to be pilgrims too. And just think, if there are many like him in our town, can you imagine how many there must be where he's from?"

"I know," Christian said, shaking his head. "God's Word says, 'He has blinded their eyes and hardened their hearts, so they can neither see with their eyes, nor understand with their hearts, nor turn—and I would heal them.'"[208]

Seeing that they had created some distance between themselves and Ignorance, Christian said, "Now that we're by ourselves, what do you think about people like Ignorance? Do you think they grasp the seriousness of their sinful condition and experience godly fear?"

---

[208] John 12:40

Hopeful nudged Christian with a smile. "Since you're the more mature and experienced Christian, I would prefer you answer that question."

Christian smiled back and then gathered his thoughts. "Well, in my opinion, I would say that sometimes people like Ignorance might experience conviction of sin followed by the fear of God. Being spiritually blind, they do not understand that such convictions are for their good, so they desperately try to suppress them while at the same time convincing themselves that their hearts are good."

Hopeful nodded. "I agree with your opinion, for the fear of God is a good motivator at the beginning of a pilgrimage to encourage people to do the right thing."

"Without a doubt, this is what happens but only when the fear of God is right and true," said Christian. "For God's Word says, 'The fear of the Lord is the beginning of wisdom.'"[209]

"How would you identify a fear of God that is right and true?" Hopeful asked.

"I would say that you could identify it in three ways," Christian said. "First, it begins with a serious concern for our sin that helps us see the need for a savior. Then, it motivates us to quickly turn to Christ as our only hope for salvation. And finally, it instills and maintains in us a great reverence for God, His Word, and His ways. This reverence keeps us mindful of God's presence so that we would be careful in turning our affections to the right or the left or to do anything that may dishonor God, break its peace, grieve the Spirit, or give God's enemies a reason to speak scornfully of Him and His kingdom."

"Well said! I believe you've spoken the truth," Hopeful said as he stopped walking and turned his attention to their surroundings. "Are we close to passing through the Enchanted

---

[209] Psalm 111:10

Ground yet?"

"Why do you ask?" Christian said with his eyebrows raised. "Are you tired of this conversation?"

"Heavens no!" replied Hopeful, a little embarrassed. "I would just like to know where we are."

"We've got a little more than two miles left to go," Christian said, pointing out in the distance. "Nevertheless, let's return to our discussion."

As they picked their pace back up, Christian continued, "Now, in general, the ignorant do not understand that these convictions of sin, which cause them to fear, are for their good, so they try to suppress them."

Hopeful was curious. "Yes, but how do they try to suppress their fears?"

Christian said, "Well, I can think of four ways.

"For one, they think their fear is from the devil when actually it's the work of God, so they resist the fear lest they be defeated.

"Also, they think their fear will undermine their faith when, unfortunately for these poor misled souls, they have no faith to begin with! So they harden their hearts against it.

"Some even presume they should have no fear, and so despite their convictions, they brazenly ignore them.

"Still others see fear as making them weak and less sure of themselves rather than spiritually strong and pious, so they resist the fear in an effort to appear self-righteous."

Hopeful lifted his hands. "I confess to knowing something of this myself because before I knew the truth, I used to be just as bad."

Seeing that they had covered that topic thoroughly, Christian said, "Well, let's leave our neighbor Ignorance to himself and move on to another interesting topic of conversation."

Hopeful wholeheartedly agreed. "But still, you should begin with a suggestion."

"Well then," said Christian, "about ten years ago, did you know a man named Temporary who lived near Vanity Fair? At one time, he was determined to become a pilgrim and was very passionate about religion back then."

"Know him!" Hopeful exclaimed. "Yes, I most certainly did. He lived in Graceless, a town that lies not more than two miles away from Honesty, and he lived next door to a man named Turnback."

"Yes, and he actually lived under the same roof with Turnback," said Christian. "Well, at one time, his life was very much awakened spiritually, and I believe he received some conviction of his sins to the point where he became overwhelmed with the consequences that were due for them."

"I believe you're right," Hopeful said. "My house was not more than three miles from Temporary's, and he would often come to me weeping over his sin. Honestly, I felt sorry for the man, but I was not altogether without hope for him. However, as you know, not everyone who cries, 'Lord, Lord!' is a true believer."

Christian nodded. "He told me once that he was determined to go on a pilgrimage just as we are now. But before long, he became friends with a man named Save-self, and after that, he began to treat me like a stranger and distanced himself from me."

"Since we're talking about Temporary," said Hopeful, "let's see if we can figure out the reason for his sudden backsliding, as well as others like him."

Christian thought this was an excellent idea. "Yes, but this time you be the one to begin."

Hopeful thought for a moment. "Well, in my opinion, there

are four reasons for backsliding.

"First, even though the consciences of such people have been temporarily awakened spiritually, their minds are not yet changed. Therefore, when the power of guilt wears off so does their desire to pursue holiness, and then they return to their former sinful ways. We see this illustrated in a sick dog that vomits what he has eaten. He does not vomit because he has a free mind, if it can be said that a dog has a free mind, but rather because his stomach is upset. But once he is no longer sick and his stomach feels better, the desire for what he has vomited returns, and he licks it all up. And so that which is written is true: 'The dog returns to his own vomit.'[210]

"This is like the person who initially is enthusiastic for Heaven but only because their fear and shame were strong and they sensed the torments of Hell. But as their fear and shame diminish, so does their desire to pursue holiness. Then, over time, when their fear and shame are gone, and their desires for Heaven and happiness die, they return to their former sinful way of life.

"The second reason for backsliding is that people have unreasonable fears that overwhelm, as when they begin to fear man more than God, as is written, 'For the fear of man will prove to be a snare.'[211] So even though they appear to be enthusiastic for Heaven so long as the flames of Hell are real to them, when that terror has passed, they begin to have second thoughts. They begin to think that it's wise not to run the risk of losing everything—or bring themselves into unavoidable and unnecessary troubles—and so they return to their worldly ways again.

"The third reason for backsliding is their convictions that arise in a time of weakness then become a crutch in times when

---

[210] 2 Pet. 2:22
[211] Prov. 29:25

they feel confident and strong. In their pride and arrogance, they view religion as base and contemptible. Therefore, when they've lost their sense and fear of the torments of Hell and the wrath to come, they return to their former sinful ways again.

"The final reason for backsliding is they dislike feeling guilty and ashamed and prefer not to think about their wrath and judgment before it happens. Though perhaps if they could see it, and then look to Christ, it might encourage them to flee to safety with the righteous. But as I hinted before, they suppress their conviction and ignore any thoughts of guilt, shame, and the wrath of God. As soon as they are rid of those feelings, they gladly harden their hearts and choose ways that will harden them even more."

Christian nodded. "You're pretty close to the heart of the matter, which, at the root, is a backslider's inability to truly change their mind and will. They are like a criminal that stands scared and trembling before the judge. He appears to repent with all his heart, but his motivation is his fear of the noose, not any true remorse for his crime. This is evident once he's set free and returns to a life of thievery and dishonesty. However, if his mind and heart were truly changed, he would live differently."

"Now that I've shared with you my thoughts regarding backsliding, please share with me your thoughts on the progression of sin that causes people like Temporary to begin to backslide."

"Gladly," said Christian as he started to list his reasons one at a time.

"First, they stop thinking about anything that reminds them of God, death, and the judgment to come and instead, focus on thoughts that produce pleasure and comfort.

"They give up any pretense of acting like a Christian in their personal life by neglecting prayer, giving in to temptation, and not feeling any grief over sin.

"Then they avoid the company of joyful, vibrant, and mature Christians that are sharing personal testimonies and asking questions.

"From there, they become less enthusiastic about church attendance and no longer listen to preaching or the public reading of God's Word or participate in corporate worship.

"To justify their actions, they start to nitpick and look for faults in the lives of other Christians. Their evil intent is to discredit religion and to provide an excuse for avoiding church.

"Then they begin to find friendship and belonging by surrounding themselves with sinful, immoral, and godless people, who just lead them further into sin.

"Eventually, they give in to immoral and ungodly conversations in their personal lives, hoping to discover others with whom they can relate and find encouragement as well as who will not put them down.

"Emboldened and unrestrained by godly influences, they now begin to sin more openly and excuse and rationalize their sins.

"And then, with their hearts now hardened, they reveal themselves for what they truly are—worse off than they were before they professed faith in Christ. Unless a miracle of grace prevents it, they will eternally perish in their own deceptions."

Chapter Twelve
The Country of Beulah

Now I saw in my dream that Christian and Hopeful were beyond the Enchanted Ground and had now entered the country of Beulah. Since the Way went directly through it, they stopped to refresh themselves for a while. The air there was very sweet and pleasant, and they listened to the singing of the birds, watched beautiful new flowers appear every day, and listened to the song of the turtledove.

The sun was shining day and night, and they were beyond the Valley of the Shadow of Death as well as the reach of Giant Despair. In fact, you could not so much as even see Doubting Castle from there. However, they were within sight of the Celestial City and met some of those that lived there. In this land, the angels frequently walked because it was located on the very borders of Heaven. Also, in this land, the contract between the Bride and the Bridegroom was renewed. Yes, here, "As the bridegroom rejoices over the bride, so does their God rejoice over them."[212]

In this land, they had no lack of grain and wine, for they reaped more than they could have ever possibly imagined receiving throughout their entire pilgrimage.

---

[212] Isa. 62:5

Here they heard loud voices from outside of the city saying, "Say to the daughter of Zion, Behold, your salvation comes! Behold, His reward is with Him!" And all the inhabitants of the country called them "the holy People, the redeemed of the Lord, sought out." They walked in this land rejoicing more than they had during any other part of their journey.

As they drew closer to the Celestial City, they had a more perfect view of it. It was built of pearls and precious stones, and the streets were paved with pure gold. The natural glory of the city and the reflection of the sunbeams upon it made both Christian and Hopeful homesick for it. They stood for a while, crying out in pain, "If you see my Beloved, tell Him that I'm love sick."[213]

After being strengthened some and better able to endure their sickness, they walked on their way and came nearer and nearer to the Celestial City. On either side, there were orchards, vineyards, and gardens, and their gates opened into the highway.

When they had come closer to these places, they found the Gardener standing in the path, so they asked him, "Who do these beautiful vineyards and gardens belong to?"

The Gardener answered, "They are the King's gardens and are planted here for His own pleasure as well as the comfort and refreshment of pilgrims."

The Gardener led them into the vineyards and told them to eat all the fruit and grapes they wanted.[214] He also showed them the King's walkways and the shaded areas that He enjoyed. Then they laid down and slept in perfect peace for a while.

Now I noticed in my dream that Christian and Hopeful talked more in their sleep at this time than at any other time in

---

[213] Song of Sol. 2:5, 5:8
[214] Deut. 23:24

all their journey. As I was wondering why, the Gardener said to me, "Why are you wondering about this matter? It's the nature of the fruit of the grapes of these vineyards to go down so sweetly as to cause the lips of those who are asleep to speak of the glories that await them."[215]

[215] Song of Sol. 7:9

The River of Death

I saw that when they awoke, they prepared themselves to go up to the Celestial City, but as I said before, the reflections of the sun on the city of pure gold were so extremely glorious that they could not face it directly, at least not yet. Instead, they used an instrument made specifically for that purpose.[216]

As they moved forward, they met two men dressed in clothes shining like gold and whose faces glowed radiantly. These angels asked the pilgrims where they came from, and they told them. They also asked them where they had visited and what difficulties, dangers, comforts, and pleasures they had encountered. Christian and Hopeful told them about their adventures along the Way.

Then the angels said, "You have just two more difficulties to overcome before you can gain entrance into the City."

Christian and Hopeful asked, "Will you guide us the rest of the way?"

The angels were willing to assist but told them, "You must complete the journey by your own faith."

I saw in my dream that they traveled together until they came in sight of the gate of the City. Between them and the gate was a very deep river with no bridge to cross over to the

---

[216] Rev. 21:18, 2 Cor. 3:18

other side. The pilgrims were stunned by the sight of the daunting and formidable river, but the angels said, "You must go through this river or else you cannot arrive at the gate of the City."

The pilgrims asked, "Is there any other way to the gate?"

"Yes," they answered, "but no one has been allowed to travel that way since the foundation of the world except for two men, Enoch and Elijah. No others will be allowed until the last trumpet sounds."

Then the pilgrims began to lose heart, especially Christian. They looked around but found no easier route that would allow them to avoid the river, so they asked, "Is the water all the same depth?"

The angels replied, "No." They offered no further guidance on the matter except to say, "You'll find it deeper or shallower according to your trust in the King of this place."

Seeing no other option, the pilgrims decided to press forward and enter the water. Immediately, Christian began to sink and cried out to his good friend Hopeful, "I'm sinking in deep waters! The billows are rolling over my head, and all the waves are crashing down on me!"

Hopeful replied, "Be courageous, my brother, for I feel the bottom, and it's firm!"

But Christian continued to panic and spluttered, "The sorrows of death have totally surrounded me! I will not see the land that flows with milk and honey!"

And with that, a great darkness and a sense of horror fell over Christian so that he could not see anything ahead of him. To a large degree, he lost his senses and could not remember or talk clearly about any of the blessings or encouragement he had experienced while traveling on his pilgrimage.

Rather, everything he said revealed terrifying thoughts and fears that he would die in that river and never gain entrance into the Celestial City. The two angels, who stood by, observed that he was haunted with thoughts of sins he had committed, both before and after he became a pilgrim, as well as disturbing visions of demons and evil spirits. His words reflected this over and over again.

Hopeful struggled to keep his brother's head above water. Sometimes Christian would come close to drowning, and then, after a while, he would rise to the surface again, almost dead. Hopeful tried his best to comfort him, calling out, "Brother, I see the gate and men standing by to receive us!"

But Christian would answer dolefully, "It's you…it's you they are waiting for! You have been hopeful ever since I knew you!"

"And so have you," responded Hopeful, doing his best to encourage his friend.

"Ah, brother!" said Christian, gasping for air. "Surely if I were right with the King, He would come to my rescue. But on account of my sins, He has brought me into the snare and abandoned me."

"My brother," Hopeful pleaded, "you have quite forgotten the Scripture where it speaks of the wicked: 'There are no pains in their death, but their strength is firm. They are not troubled as other men, neither are they plagued like other men.'[217]

"These troubles and distresses that you're experiencing in these waters are not indicating that God has abandoned you. Rather, they are sent to test you to see whether or not you will recall the promises of God and rely on Him in your present trial."

Hopeful noticed that Christian was in deep thought, so he continued to speak. "Be courageous! Jesus Christ makes you

---

[217] Ps. 73:4–5

whole."

With that, Christian exclaimed with a loud voice, "Oh, I see Him again and He tells me, "When you pass through the waters—I will be with you. When you go through the rivers—they will not overflow you!'"[218]

Suddenly, they both became courageous, and after that, the enemy was as still as a stone and could no longer hinder them. Christian now found solid ground to stand on, and the two of them waded through the rest of the shallow river and crossed over.

---

[218] Is. 43:2

A Heavenly Welcome

A s they arrived on the other side of the river bank, once again Christian and Hopeful saw the two angels waiting to welcome them as they came out of the river. The angels greeted them, saying, "We are ministering spirits sent forth to serve those who will be heirs of salvation." Then they all proceeded toward the gate.

Now, it is worth noting that the City stood upon a mighty hill, but the pilgrims ascended that hill with ease because they had the two angels lead them up by holding their arms. Plus, they had left their mortal clothes behind them in the river, for although they went in the river with them, they came out without them.

They continued to climb with much agility and speed, even though the foundation upon which the city was built was higher than the clouds. They went up through the regions of the air, sweetly talking as they went, being comforted because they had safely crossed the river and had such glorious companions to escort them.

They talked with the angels about the splendor of the place. The angels told the pilgrims that the beauty and glory of it were simply inexpressible. "In Mount Zion," the angels said, "you'll find the heavenly Jerusalem, the innumerable company of angels, and the spirits of just men made perfect."[219]

---

[219] Heb. 12:22–23

"You're going now," they said, "to the paradise of God, where you'll see the Tree of Life and eat of the never-fading fruits! When you arrive, you'll be given white robes, and you'll walk and talk with the King every day through all eternity!"[220]

The angels continued, "There you will never again see such things as you saw when you were in the lower region upon Earth, including sorrow, sickness, affliction, and death, for the former things are passed away.[221] Rather, you are going now to Abraham, to Isaac, and to Jacob and to the prophets—men whom God has taken away from the evil to come and who are now at rest, each one walking in his righteousness."

"What will we do in the holy City?" Christian and Hopeful asked.

"There you will receive the comforts from all your toil and have joy in place of your sorrow," the angels answered. "You will reap what you have sown, even the fruit of all your prayers, tears, and sufferings for the King along the Way.[222] In that place, you will wear crowns of gold and enjoy the perpetual sight and vision of the Holy One, for there you will see Him as He is.[223]

"You will also serve the one whom you desired to serve in the world with much difficulty because of the weakness of your flesh. You will do so with continuous praise, shouting, and thanksgiving. There your eyes will be delighted with seeing Him and your ears with hearing the pleasant voice of the Mighty One. There you will enjoy your friends again, who arrived before you, and in the same way, you will welcome everyone with joy who follows you into the holy place.

---

[220] Rev. 2:7, 3:4–5, 22:5
[221] Rev. 21:4
[222] Gal. 6:7–8
[223] 1 John 3:2

"There also you will be clothed with glory and majesty and appropriately equipped to ride out with the King of Glory when He comes in the clouds with the sound of the trumpet upon the wings of the wind, and you will come with Him. When He sits upon the throne of judgment, you will sit by Him, and when He passes sentence upon all the workers of iniquity, whether angels or men, you also will have a voice in that judgment because they were both His and your enemies. Also, when He again returns to the City, you will go with Him with the sound of a trumpet and be with Him forever."[224]

Now, as they were drawing near the gate, a company of the heavenly host came out to meet them. To this multitude the two angels said, "These are the men who have loved our Lord when they were in the world, and they have left all for His holy name. He has sent us to fetch them, and we have brought them this far on their desired journey so that they now may go in and look their Redeemer in the face with joy."

Then the heavenly host gave a great shout, saying, "Blessed are they who are called to the marriage supper of the Lamb!"[225]

At this time, several of the King's trumpeters also came out to meet them. They had white shining clothes, and with loud, melodious noises, they made even the heavens to echo with their sound. These trumpeters greeted Christian and Hopeful with ten thousand welcomes from the world, and they did this with shouting and the sound of the trumpets.

Afterward, the angels surrounded them on every side. Some went in front, some went behind, and some went on the right and left as a guard through the upper regions. As they went, they continued making melodious noise and lofty notes. To all who could see, it was as if Heaven itself came down to meet them.

---

[224] 1 Thess. 4:14–17, Jude 14–15, Dan. 7:9–10, 1 Cor. 6:2–3
[225] Rev. 19:9

As they walked on together, these trumpeters would often, with joyful sound, combine their music with looks and gestures to signify to Christian and Hopeful just how welcome the pilgrims were and how happy they were to meet them. Surrounded by the angels and the sound of their melodious music, it was as if these two pilgrims were already in Heaven.

Here they also had a better view of the City itself, and they thought they heard all the bells ringing in the City to welcome them inside. But above all, they were consumed with warm and joyful thoughts about living there for all eternity with such heavenly company. Oh, with what language or pen could they express their glorious joy as they arrived at the gate?

When they came up to the gate, there was inscribed over it in letters of gold, "Blessed are those who obey His commandments that they may have the right to the Tree of Life and may enter in through the gates into the City."

Then I saw in my dream that the angels told them to call out at the gate. When they did, some looked over the gate, namely Enoch, Moses, and Elijah, and they were told, "These pilgrims have come from the City of Destruction for the love they have for the King of this place."

Then each pilgrim handed in their certificate, which they had kept in their chest pocket and had received at the beginning of their journey. These were carried in to the King, who, when He read them, asked, "Where are these men?"

"They are standing outside the gate" was the answer.

Then the King commanded the gate to be opened and declared, "The righteous nation that keeps the truth may enter in."[226]

Now I saw in my dream that Christian and Hopeful went in the gate, and as they entered, they were suddenly transfigured

---

[226] Is. 26:2

and arrayed in clothes that shone like gold. Some of the inhabitants of the City met them and provided harps and crowns. The harps were given for worship, and the crowns were given as a token of honor.

Then I heard in my dream all the bells in the city ring again for joy and that it was said to the pilgrims, "Enter into the joy of your Lord!"

I also heard Christian and Hopeful sing with a loud voice, saying, "Blessing, and honor, and glory, and power to Him who sits upon the throne and to the Lamb, forever and ever!"

Just as the gates were opened to let the men inside, I looked in after them and witnessed the City shining like the sun! The streets were also paved with gold, and many men walked on them with crowns on their heads, palms in their hands, and golden harps to sing praises with forever.

There were also some angelic beings with wings that responded in never-ending praise, saying, "Holy, holy, holy is the Lord!" Then I watched them shut the gates and wished that I, too, was among them.

While I was watching all of this happen, I turned my head to look back and saw Ignorance come up to the riverbank. He soon crossed over without half the difficulty Christian and Hopeful had met. As it turned out, the one called Vain-Hope, a ferryman, was there and helped Ignorance cross the river.

Then I saw Ignorance ascend the hill, just like the others, to arrive at the gate of the Celestial City—only he came alone, and no one met him to offer the least bit of encouragement.

When he reached the gate, he looked up to the writing that was inscribed above it and began to knock, assuming he would quickly be permitted entrance. But the men peered over the top of the gate and asked, "Where did you come from, and what is it that you desire?"

He replied, "I've eaten and drunk in the presence of the

King, and He has taught in our streets."

Then they asked him for his certificate so that they might go in and show it to the King. Ignorance fumbled in his chest pocket but found nothing.

The men at the gate said, "Do you not have a certificate?" Ignorance just stood there speechless.

The men informed the King that Ignorance was at the gate, but He would not come down to see him. Instead, He commanded the two angels, who had welcomed Christian and Hopeful to the City, to go out and take Ignorance, bind his hands and feet, and cast him out.

The angels took Ignorance up and carried him through the air to the door that I had seen in the side of the hill below the Delectable Mountains and put him in there. Then I realized that there was a way to Hell, even from the very gate of Heaven, as well as from the City of Destruction.

So I awoke and saw that it was a dream!

The Conclusion

Now reader, I have told my dream to you,
See if you can interpret it to me,
Or to yourself, or neighbor; but pay attention
Of misinterpreting; for that, instead
Of doing good, will but yourself abuse:
By misinterpreting evil ensues.

Pay attention also, that you do not become extreme,
In playing with the outside of my dream;
Nor let my figure, or similitude,
Put you into a laughter or start a feud;
Leave this for boys and fools; but as for you,
Do yourself the substance of my matter see.

Open the curtains, look within my veil;
Turn up my metaphors and do not fail:
If you seek them, such things to find,
As will be helpful to an honest mind.

What of my waste you find there, be bold,
To throw away, but yet preserve the gold.
What if my apple be wrapped up in ore?
None throws away the apple for the core

But if you should cast all away as vain,
I know not but it will make me dream again.

Leave a Review

Thank you again for reading this book! I hope and pray that in some way it encouraged you (and your group) to grow closer to Christ.

If you enjoyed this book, I would appreciate your leaving an honest review for the book and study on Amazon! Your review will help others know if this study is right for them and their small group.

It's easy and will only take a minute. Just search for "The Pilgrim's Progress, Alan Vermilye" on Amazon. Click on the product in the search results, and then click on reviews.

I would also love to hear from you! Drop me a note by visiting me at www.BrownChairBooks.com and clicking on "Contact."

Thank you and God bless!

Alan

Other Studies from Brown Chair Books

On the following pages, you'll descriptions and reviews from some of our other Bible studies.

www.BrownChairBooks.com

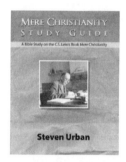
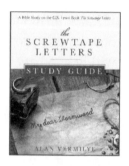

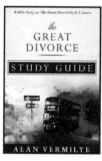

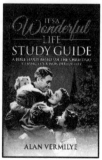

MERE CHRISTIANITY STUDY GUIDE
A Bible Study on the C.S. Lewis Book *Mere Christianity*
By Steven Urban

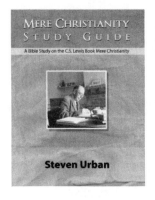

Steven Urban

Mere Christianity Study Guide takes participants through a study of C.S. Lewis's classic *Mere Christianity*. Yet despite its recognition as a "classic," there is surprisingly little available today in terms of a serious study course.

This 12-week Bible study digs deep into each chapter and, in turn, into Lewis's thoughts. Perfect for small group sessions, this interactive workbook includes daily, individual study as well as a complete appendix and commentary to supplement and further clarify certain topics. Multiple week format options are also included.

What others are saying:

This study guide is more than just a guide to C.S Lewis' Mere Christianity; it is a guide to Christianity itself. – Crystal

Wow! What a lot of insight and food for thought! Perfect supplement to Mere Christianity. *I think Mr. Lewis himself would approve.* – Laurie

Our group is in the middle of studying Mere Christianity, *and I have found this guide to be invaluable.*
– Angela

THE SCREWTAPE LETTERS STUDY GUIDE
A Bible Study on the C.S. Lewis Book
The Screwtape Letters
By Alan Vermilye

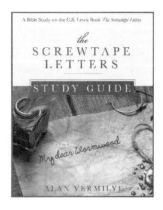

The Screwtape Letters Study Guide takes participants through a study of C.S. Lewis's classic, *The Screwtape Letters*.

This Bible study digs deep into each letter from Screwtape, an undersecretary in the lowerarchy of Hell, to his incompetent nephew Wormwood, a junior devil. Perfect for small group sessions, this interactive workbook includes daily, individual study with a complete answer guide available online.

Designed as a 12-week study, multiple-week format options are also included.

What others are saying:

This book and study creates a positive reinforcement on fighting that spiritual battle in life. Great read, great study guide! – Lester

This study guide was a wonderful way for our group to work through The Screwtape Letters*!* – Becky

Use this study guide for a fresh "seeing" of The Screwtape Letters*!* – William

THE GREAT DIVORCE STUDY GUIDE
A Bible Study on the C.S. Lewis Book *The Great Divorce*
By Alan Vermilye

The Great Divorce Study Guide is an eight-week Bible study on the C.S. Lewis classic, *The Great Divorce*. Perfect for small groups or individual study, each weekly study session applies a biblical framework to the concepts found in each chapter of the book. Although intriguing and entertaining, much of Lewis's writings can be difficult to grasp.

The Great Divorce Study Guide will guide you through each one of Lewis's masterful metaphors to a better understanding of the key concepts of the book, the supporting Bible passages, and the relevance to our world today. Each study question is ideal for group discussion, and answers to each question are available online.

What others are saying:

To my knowledge, there have not been many study guides for either of these, so to see this new one on The Great Divorce *(both electronic and print) is a welcome sight!* – Richard

I recommend The Great Divorce Study Guide *to anyone or any group wishing to delve more deeply into the question, why would anyone choose hell over heaven!* – Ruth

THE PROBLEM OF PAIN STUDY GUIDE
A Bible Study on the C.S. Lewis Book *The Problem of Pain*
By Alan Vermilye

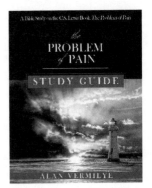

In his book, *The Problem of Pain*, C.S. Lewis's philosophical approach to why we experience pain can be confusing at times. *The Problem of Pain Study Guide* breaks down each chapter into easy-to-understand questions and commentary to help you find meaning and hope amid the pain.

The Problem of Pain Study Guide expands upon Lewis's elegant and thoughtful work, where he seeks to understand how a loving, good, and powerful God can possibly coexist with the pain and suffering that is so pervasive in the world and in our lives. As Christ-followers we might expect the world to be just, fair, and less painful, but it is not. This is the problem of pain.

What others are saying:

Many thanks for lending me a helping hand with one of the greatest thinkers of all time! – Adrienne

The questions posed range from very straightforward (to help the reader grasp main concepts) to more probing (to facilitate personal application), while perhaps the greatest benefit they supply is their tie-in of coordinating scriptures that may not always be apparent to the reader. – Sphinn

A CHRISTMAS CAROL STUDY GUIDE
Book and Bible Study Based on *A Christmas Carol*
By Alan Vermilye

A Christmas Carol Book and Bible Study Guide includes the entire book of this Dickens classic as well as Bible study discussion questions for each chapter, Scripture references, and related commentary.

Detailed character sketches and an easy-to-read book summary provide deep insights into each character while examining the book's themes of greed, isolation, guilt, blame, compassion, generosity, transformation, forgiveness, and, finally, redemption. To help with those more difficult discussion questions, a complete answer guide is available for free online.

What others are saying:

The study is perfect for this time of the year, turning our focus to the reason for the season—Jesus—and the gift of redemption we have through him. – Connie

I used this for an adult Sunday School class. We all loved it! – John

This study is wonderful! – Lori

I found this a refreshing look at the Bible through the eyes of Ebenezer Scrooge's life. – Lynelle

IT'S A WONDERFUL STUDY GUIDE

A Bible Study Based on the Christmas Classic *It's a Wonderful Life*
By Alan Vermilye

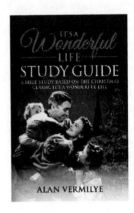

It's a Wonderful Life is one of the most popular and heart-warming films ever made. It's near-universal appeal and association with Christmas has provided a rich story of redemption that has inspired generations for decades.

It's a Wonderful Life Study Guide examines this beloved holiday classic and reminds us how easily we can become distracted from what is truly meaningful in life. This five-week Bible study experience comes complete with discussion questions for each session, Scripture references, detailed character sketches, movie summary, and related commentary. In addition, a complete answer guide and video segments for each session are available for free online.

What others are saying:

Thank you, Alan, for the unforgettable experience. Your book has prompted me to see and learn much more than merely enjoying the film, It's a Wonderful Life. – Er Jwee

The questions got us all thinking, and the answers provided were insightful and encouraging. I would definitely encourage Home Groups to study this! – Jill

It's a Wonderful Life Study Guide *by Alan Vermilye is intelligent, innovative, interesting, involving, insightful, and inspirational.* – Paul